BTEC Level 3 National Study Skills Guide in Land and Environment

Welcome to your Study Skills Guide! You can make it your own – start by adding your personal and course details below...

Learner's name: _____

BTEC course title: _____

Date started: _____

Mandatory units:

_____

_____

_____

Optional units:

_____

_____

_____

Centre name: _____

Centre address:

_____

_____

_____

Tutor's name: _____

Published by Pearson Education Limited, a company incorporated in England and Wales, having its registered office at Edinburgh Gate, Harlow, Essex, CM20 2JE. Registered company number: 872828

Edexcel is a registered trademark of Edexcel Limited

Text © Pearson Education Limited 2010

First published 2010

19 18

12 11

British Library Cataloguing in Publication Data

A catalogue record for this book is available from the British Library

ISBN 978 1 84690 927 6

Typeset and edited by DSM Partnership
Cover design by Visual Philosophy, created by eMC Design
Cover photo/illustration © Agripicture Images/Peter Dean
Printed and bound by L.E.G.O. S.p.A. Lavis (TN) - Italy

Acknowledgements

The publisher would like to thank the following for their kind permission to reproduce their photographs:
(Key: b-bottom; c-centre; l-left; r-right; t-top)

Alamy Images: Angela Hampton Picture Library 19, Claudia Wiens 66; **Corbis**: 76; Tom Goss: 44, 50l, 50r, 51l, 51r; **iStockphoto**: David H. Lewis 16, Chris Schmidt 33, Leah Sisson 10; **Pearson Education Ltd**: Steve Shott 28, Ian Wedgewood 59

All other images © Pearson Education

Every effort has been made to trace the copyright holders and we apologise in advance for any unintentional omissions. We would be pleased to insert the appropriate acknowledgement in any subsequent edition of this publication.

Websites

Go to www.pearsonhotlinks.co.uk to gain access to the relevant website links and information on how they can aid your studies. When you access the site, search for either the title BTEC Level 3 National Study Skills Guide in Land and Environment or ISBN 9781846909276.

Disclaimer

This material has been published on behalf of Edexcel and offers high-quality support for the delivery of Edexcel qualifications.

This does not mean that the material is essential to achieve any Edexcel qualification, nor does it mean that it is the only suitable material available to support any Edexcel qualification. Edexcel material will not be used verbatim in setting any Edexcel examination or assessment. Any resource lists produced by Edexcel shall include this and other appropriate resources.

Copies of official specifications for all Edexcel qualifications may be found on the Edexcel website: www.edexcel.com

Contents

Popular progression pathways

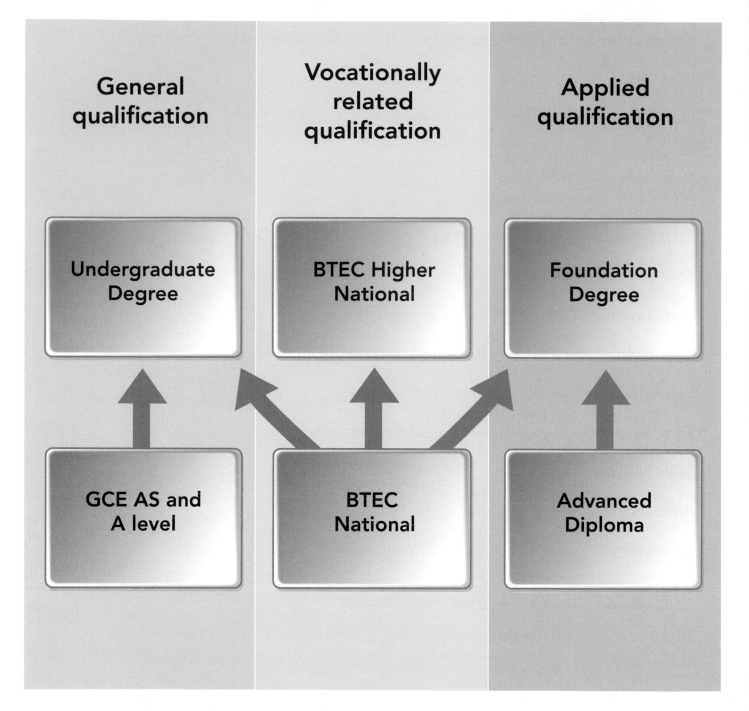

Ten steps to success in your BTEC Level 3 National

This Study Skills Guide has been written to help you achieve the best result possible on your BTEC Level 3 National course. At the start of a new course you may feel both quite excited but also a little apprehensive. Taking a BTEC Level 3 National qualification has many benefits and is a major stepping stone towards your future career. Using this Study Skills Guide will help you get the most out of your course from the start.

> **TOP TIP**
>
> Use this Study Skills Guide at your own pace. Dip in to find what you need. Look back at it if you have a problem or query.

During **induction** sessions at the start of your course, your tutor will explain important information, but it can be difficult to remember everything and that's when you'll find this Study Skills Guide invaluable. Look at it whenever you want to check anything related to your course. It provides all the essential facts you need and has a Useful terms section to explain specialist terms, words and phrases, including some that you will see highlighted in this book in bold type.

This Study Skills Guide covers the skills you'll need to do well in your course – such as managing your time, researching and analysing information and preparing a presentation.

- Use **Top tips** to make your life easier as you go.
- Use **Key points** to help you to stay focused on the essentials.
- Use **Action points** to check what you need to know or do now.
- Use **Case studies** to relate information to your chosen sector and vocational area.
- Use **Activities** to test your knowledge and skills.
- Use the **Useful terms** section to check the meaning of specialist terms.

This Study Skills Guide is divided into ten steps, each relating to a key aspect of your studies, from understanding assessment to time management to maximising opportunities. Concentrate on getting things right one step at a time. Thousands of learners have achieved BTEC Level 3 National qualifications and are now studying for a degree, or building a successful career at work. Using this Study Skills Guide, and believing in your own abilities, will help you achieve your future goals, too.

Introduction to the land and environment sector

Cradling a newborn lamb in your arms; watching a dragonfly emerge from a pond's edge, enjoying a red, juicy strawberry that you've grown yourself; releasing a rescued lion back into the open savannah; planting trees that will provide the timber and fuel for future generations; watching a horse that you raised win the Grand National – these are some of the rewarding aspects of working in the land and environment sector.

A BTEC Level 3 National in one of the land and environment subjects can lead to a fascinating career. You can learn more about the world around you, take on new challenges, and experience extraordinary events. Each year thousands of people leave well-established careers to take up new ones in the countryside. And you can join them – straight from school.

Of course, it's not just about the countryside, nor is it restricted to the UK. A BTEC Level 3 National in one of the land and environment subjects can open doors to a range of opportunities. Let's just think about some of the things that rely upon the skills provided by people who started their life after school studying one of the BTEC Nationals in the land and environment sector.

Do you like sports? What about football, golf or tennis? Who do you think keeps the pitch in top condition at the Emirates Stadium or the Millennium Stadium, or the greens at St. Andrews, or those all-important make-or-break lines precisely marked at Wimbledon? You don't have to be a sporting star to work at iconic sporting venues around the world.

However, there's more to grasses than lawns. All the major grains are grasses, too. Life would not be the same if we didn't have wheat to make bread, or maize or oats for breakfast cereals and porridge.

But grasses aren't the only things you can grow. What about fruits and vegetables – big-scale, small-scale; organic, conventional; private enterprise or community co-operative? We all need to eat, and food farming is crucial to our basic needs.

You may be interested in animals – big ones, little ones, tame and not-so-tame. There are possibilities for studying tigers at a zoo, safari park or in northern India; dogs at a local kennels; cats at a rescue centre; hawks, eagles and owls in a raptor sanctuary; rare native smooth snakes or sand lizards on a heathland site; dairy cows on your own farm; or a giant octopus at a marine centre.

With the prevalence of screens (computers, phones, televisions) in our daily lives, some experts are predicting a resurgence of demand for work in the outdoors.

Look at the diagram below for where a BTEC National in land and environment subjects can lead to.

BTEC Nationals in Land and Environment				
Horticulture	Horse Management	Animal Care	Agriculture	Countryside Management and Forestry
CAREERS	**CAREERS**	**CAREERS**	**CAREERS**	**CAREERS**
Sports Field Manager	Stables Manager	Animal Welfare Inspector	Dairy Farmer	Countryside Ranger
Garden Designer	Horse Trainer	Pet Shop Manager	Agricultural Contractor	Nature Reserve Warden
Fruit & Veg Grower	Race Horse Breeder		Livestock Manager	Tree Surgeon

Level 3 skills for the land and environment sector

Having identified your ideal job, you have to think about how you will succeed in getting it. You will need to gain skills, and that's where BTEC Nationals in Land and Environment come in.

First and foremost, these will be practical skills, and they cover just about everything:

- handling large and small animals safely
- firing a rifle or shotgun accurately
- driving an all-terrain vehicle
- designing and constructing fences, pens and other animal enclosures
- utilising up-to-date technology for growing fruit, vegetables and other crops
- safely felling a hazardous tree in a built-up area using chainsaws, harnesses and climbing ropes
- safely managing and riding horses
- creating the perfect flower arrangement
- identifying trees, flowers, birds and mammals.

However, practical skills will only get you so far. Consider these activities:

A leading a guided walk in the countryside

B designing new dog kennels

C creating an information board for an animal park.

Use the table below to make a note of other skills that might be required.

Task	Practical skills	Other skills
A. Guided walk	Identification of natural features Knowledge of landscape history Understanding of ecosystems	
B. Dog kennels	Understanding of dog breeds Knowledge of dog living requirements Understanding of legal requirements regarding animal living conditions	
C. Information board	Identification of animal species and breeds Knowledge of life histories of different animals	

What skills did you think of? The following are some of the other skills you may have considered.

A Guided walk. You may have been on a guided tour when you were on a holiday or a school trip. This example is about the countryside, but it could apply anywhere, such as a museum, zoo or historic building – the principles are the same.

Situation	Skill Required
Could you hear the tour leader and understand them?	Communication – being able to project your voice to the entire group and being able to speak clearly with the right tone at the right speed.
Did they appear confident and knowledgeable?	Time management (particularly for preparation), communication and presentation skills, as well as self-knowledge. Knowing yourself allows you to be yourself and lets the real you be fully expressed.
Did they walk too slowly or too fast?	Teamwork skills are important here. In addition to knowing themselves, a good leader knows their group and its capabilities.

B Designing new dog kennels.

Situation	Skill Required
Designing the layout.	There will be a need to calculate areas, so some maths work required here. You may have access to a computer-aided design (CAD) package – your computer skills will be useful for that.
Estimating costs.	Some more maths skills here. Calculating amounts and costs. Again, much of this can be done using a spreadsheet program on a computer.

C Finally, what skills did you identify for creating an information board for an animal park? If you haven't been to an animal park, you may have seen an information board (or similar) at a zoo, a museum, an historic garden or house. They are everywhere. The question is: are they any good?

Situation	Skill Required
Was the board interesting? Did you read the whole thing or have a quick glance and move on?	Good writing skills required for this as well as presentation regarding the use of images and colour.
Did you learn something or gain a better understanding? Did it make you think about something in a different way?	Again, good writing and creative presentation skills required here.

A BTEC National in one of the land and environment subjects provides the complete package of skills that you need to embark upon the career that you want.

Step One: Understand your course and how it works

Case study: preparing for an interview

Jane has been invited for an interview as part of the application process for a BTEC Level 3 National in Horse Management. Her Dad is very supportive of her doing the course because she has found something she is really interested in, but her Mum is not so sure. At the interview, Jane wants to be ready with lots of good questions to address both her own queries and her mum's concerns.

Jane has looked through the units delivered by the centre; all of them sound interesting, but she wants to know how long she is going to be sitting in a classroom compared to the time spent caring for, handling and riding the horses. Also, there is a unit called 'Undertake Estate Skills' and she wonders what it is about and why it is important.

Jane doesn't have her own equipment and knows that buying it can be expensive. She would like to know how much riding equipment is provided by the centre and what particular items they recommend she buys for herself.

Having found out more about the content of the course, Jane prepares her final questions – these are the ones that she knows her Mum is most concerned about:

'What extra qualifications and skills will I receive as part of the course?'

'What types of jobs will this lead to?'

'Can you tell me what recent graduates are doing and where they are working?'

Being prepared is essential for any interview situation. You don't want to be sitting in a classroom in a year's time asking yourself why you are there.

Reflection point

What makes you certain that you have chosen the right course for you?

All BTEC Level 3 National qualifications are **vocational** or **work-related**. This means that you gain specific knowledge and understanding that is relevant to your chosen area. It gives you several advantages when you start work. For example, you will already know quite a lot about your chosen area, which will help you settle down more quickly. If you are already employed, you become more valuable to your employer.

Your BTEC course will prepare you for the work you want to do.

There are four types of BTEC Level 3 National qualification: Certificates, Subsidiary Diplomas, Diplomas and Extended Diplomas

	Certificate	Subsidiary Diploma	Diploma	Extended Diploma
Credit	30	60	120	180
Equivalence	1 AS level	1 A level	2 A levels	3 A levels

These qualifications are often described as **nested**. This means that they fit inside each other (rather like Russian dolls) because the same units are common to each qualification – so you can progress from one to another easily by completing more units.

TOP TIP

The structure of BTEC Level 3 National qualifications means it's easy to progress from one type to another and gain more credits, as well as to specialise in particular areas that interest you.

- Every BTEC Level 3 National qualification has a set number of **mandatory units** that all learners must complete.
- All BTEC Level 3 National qualifications include **optional units** that enable you to study particular areas in more depth.

- Some BTEC Level 3 National qualifications have **specialist pathways**, which may have additional mandatory units. These specialist pathways allow you to follow your career aims more precisely. For example, if you are studying to become an IT practitioner, you can choose pathways in software development, networking, systems support or IT and business.

- On all BTEC courses you are expected to be responsible for your own learning. Obviously your tutor will give you help and guidance when necessary but you also need to be 'self-starting' and able to use your own initiative. Ideally, you will also be able to assess how well you are doing and make improvements when necessary.

- BTEC Level 3 National grades convert to UCAS points, just like A levels, but the way you are assessed and graded on a BTEC course is different, as you will see in the next section.

Key points

- You can study part-time or full-time for your BTEC Level 3 National.

- You can do a Certificate, Subsidiary Diploma, Diploma or Extended Diploma, and progress easily from one to the other.

- You will study both mandatory units and optional units on your course.

- When you have completed your BTEC course you can get a job (or **apprenticeship**), use your qualification to develop your career and/or continue studying to degree level.

- On all BTEC Level 3 National courses, the majority of your learning is practical and vocationally focused to develop the skills you need for your chosen career.

Using the Edexcel website to find out about your course

- You can check all the details about your BTEC Level 3 National course on the Edexcel website – go to www.edexcel.com.

- Enter the title of your BTEC Level 3 National qualification in the qualifications finder.

- Now find the specification in the list of documents. This is a long document so don't try to print it. Instead, look at the information on the units you will be studying to see the main topics you will cover.

- Then save the document or bookmark the page so that you can easily refer to it again if you need to.

Action points

1 By discussing with your tutor and by exploring the Edexcel website, find out the key information about your course and use it to complete the 'Important information' form on the next page. You can refer to this form at any time to refresh your memory about any part of your studies.

a) Check whether you are studying for a BTEC Level 3 Certificate, Subsidiary Diploma, Diploma, or Extended Diploma, and find out the number of units you will be studying.

b) Find out the titles of the mandatory units you will be studying.

c) Find out the titles of the optional units and identify the ones offered at your centre.

d) Check the length of your course, and when you will be studying each unit.

e) Identify the optional units you will be taking. On some National courses you will do this at the start, while on others you may make your final decision later.

f) Find out other relevant information about your BTEC Level 3 National qualification. Your centre may have already given you details about the course structure.

g) Ask your tutor to help you to complete section 10 on the form. Depending on your course, you may be developing specific additional or personal skills – such as personal, learning and thinking skills (PLTS) and functional skills – or spending time on work experience, going on visits or doing other activities linked to your subject area.

h) Talk to your tutor about section 12 on the form as your sources of information will depend on the careers guidance and information at your centre. You may find it useful to exchange ideas with other members of your class.

IMPORTANT INFORMATION ON MY BTEC LEVEL 3 NATIONAL COURSE	
1	The title of the BTEC Level 3 National qualification I am studying is:
2	The length of my course is:
3	The total number of units I will study is:
4	The number of mandatory units I have to study is:
5	The titles of these mandatory units and the dates (or terms) when I will study them are:
6	The main topics I will learn in each mandatory unit include:

IMPORTANT INFORMATION ON MY BTEC LEVEL 3 NATIONAL COURSE	
7	The number of optional units I have to study is:
8	The titles of the optional units I will study are:
9	The main topics I will learn in each optional unit include:
10	Other important aspects of my course are:
11	After I have achieved my BTEC Level 3 National my options include:
12	Useful sources of information I can use to find out more about these options include:

2 Many learners already have information, contacts or direct experiences that relate to their course. For example, you may have a specific interest or hobby that links to a unit, such as being a St John Ambulance cadet if you are studying Public Services. Think about the relevant sources of information you already have access to and complete the table below.

MY INFORMATION SOURCES	
Experts I know	(Who they are, what they know)
My hobbies and interests	(What they are, what they involve)
My job(s)	(Past and present work and work experience, and what I did)
Programmes I like to watch	(What these are, how they relate to my course)
Magazines and/or books I read	(What these are, examples of relevant articles)
ICT sources	(My centre's intranet as well as useful websites)
Other	(Other sources relevant for my particular course and the topics I will be studying)

Activity: Choosing units

So, you think you might be interested in a BTEC National in the land and environment sector, and you think you know what is involved in doing a course? Examine the following profiles and identify units from the specification that would be of particular interest to these BTEC Level 3 National learners. Suggest five units for each scenario.

James lives on a dairy farm that has been in the family for two generations. He loves farming and would like to continue the family tradition. In addition to building up the dairy business, James is keen to improve the wildlife habitats on the farm and convert to an organic system.	1
	2
	3
	4
	5
Sarah is an animal lover, and is particularly fond of dogs. Her dream job would be to have her own kennels where she could not only look after other people's pets, but also breed and sell puppies.	1
	2
	3
	4
	5
Lisa is really frustrated with life. She has a good family and some nice friends, so superficially everything is all right, but inside she is confused. She's not that interested in the latest mobile phone or hot celeb gossip: she would like to make a difference in the world. Although she volunteers for a local green group, she wants to know more about sustainable development, growing her own organic fruits and vegetables, and how land could be better used for everybody.	1
	2
	3
	4
	5
Ever since he was little, Tim has climbed trees in the local park. Not only were the views great, but every tree presented a challenge. He recently saw a group of tree surgeons in the park removing some dangerous branches, and realised that this would be his ideal job.	1
	2
	3
	4
	5

BTEC Level 3 Nationals in Floristry offer a diverse range of units such as Historical Floristry Designs and Photography, Media, Techniques and Technology.

Step Two: Understand how you are assessed and graded

Case study: Understanding your assessmen

John is reading through some of the units for a BTEC Level 3 National in Countryside Management. He is surprised at how many different assessment methods there are. It is totally different from what he was used to at school, where he had lots of tests, exams and written work.

There are no exams – no long hours of revising trying to cram in as much information as possible, only to forget it all a few months after the exam. He notices that although there are several assignments with each unit he won't necessarily have to write lots of essays. Actually, most of the assignments are really practical. For example, for some of the pass criteria, no writing is required at all and they can be assessed by practical observation records, where the tutor observes learners doing an activity. There are also witness statements.

John is volunteering at a nearby nature reserve – the highlight of his week – and this means that the supervisor can complete a witness statement, and take some photos to show that a pass criterion has been achieved.

However, to achieve a merit or a distinction, John knows that he needs to do additional research and writing. For example, the nature reserve where he works needs a management plan so John can produce a management plan for the distinction criterion that could be used by the nature reserve. He will also be able to use this on his CV.

Reflection points

Is there anything about the BTEC assessment process you need to understand better?

Your assessment

This section looks at the importance of your assignments, how they are graded and how this converts into unit points and UCAS points. Unlike A levels, there are no externally-set final exams on a BTEC course. Even if you know this because you already have a BTEC First qualification, you should still read this section as now you will be working at a different level.

Your learning is assessed by **assignments**, set by your tutors. You will complete these throughout your course, using many different **assessment methods**, such as real-life case studies, **projects** and presentations. Some assignments may be work-based or **time-constrained** – this will depend on the vocational area you are studying.

Your assignments are based on **learning outcomes** set by Edexcel. These are listed for each unit in your course specification. You must achieve **all** the learning outcomes for each unit to pass the unit.

TOP TIP

Check the learning outcomes for each unit by referring to the course specification – go to www.edexcel.com.

Important skills to help you achieve your grades include:

- researching and analysing information (see page 63)
- using your time effectively (see page 25)
- working co-operatively as a member of a team (see page 57.)

Your grades, unit points and UCAS points

On a BTEC Level 3 National course, assessments that meet the learning outcomes are graded as pass, merit or distinction. The different grades within each unit are set out by Edexcel as **grading criteria** in a **grading grid**. These criteria identify the **higher-level skills** you must demonstrate

to achieve a higher grade (see also Step Six: Understand your assessment, on page 35).

All your assessment grades earn **unit points**. The total points you get for all your units determines your final qualification grade(s) – pass, merit or distinction. You get:

- one final grade if you are taking a Certificate or Subsidiary Diploma
- two final grades if you are taking a Diploma
- three final grades if you are taking an Extended Diploma.

Your points and overall grade(s) convert to **UCAS points**, which you need to be accepted onto a degree course. For example, if you achieve three final pass grades for your BTEC Level 3 Extended Diploma, you get 120 UCAS Tariff points. If you achieve three final distinction grades, this increases to 360 – equivalent to three GCE A levels.

Please note that all UCAS information was correct at the time of going to print, but we would advise that you check the UCAS website for the most up-to-date information. See page 96 for how to access their website.

Case study: Securing a university place

Chris and Shaheeda both want a university place and have worked hard on their BTEC Level 3 Extended Diploma course.

Chris's final score is 226 unit points, which converts to 280 UCAS Tariff points. Shaheeda has a total score of 228 unit points – just two points more – which converts to 320 UCAS points. This is because a score of between 204

and 227 unit points gives 280 UCAS points, whereas a score of 228 to 251 points gives 320 UCAS points.

Shaheeda is delighted because this increases her chances of getting a place on the degree course she wants. Chris is annoyed. He says if he had realised, he would have worked harder to get two more points on his last assignment.

You start to earn points from your first assessment, so you get many benefits from settling in quickly and doing good work from the start. Understanding how **grade boundaries** work also helps you to focus your efforts to get the best possible final grade.

You will be able to discuss your learning experiences, your personal progress and the

achievement of your learning objectives in **individual tutorials** with your tutor. These enable you to monitor your progress and overcome temporary difficulties. You can also talk about any worries you have. Your tutor is one of your most important resources and a tutorial gives you their undivided attention.

You can talk through any questions or problems in your tutorials.

Key points

- Your learning is assessed in a variety of ways, such as by assignments, projects and real-life case studies.

- You need to demonstrate specific knowledge and skills to achieve the learning outcomes set by Edexcel. You must achieve all the grading criteria to pass a unit.

- The grading criteria for pass, merit and distinction are shown in a grading grid for the unit. Higher-level skills are needed for higher grades.

- The assessment grades of pass, merit and distinction convert to unit points. The total unit points you receive for the course determines your final overall grade(s) and UCAS points.

TOP TIP

It's always tempting to spend longer on work you like doing and are good at, but focusing on improving your weak areas will do more to boost your overall grade(s).

Action points

1 Find out more about your own course by carrying out this activity.

a) Find the learning outcomes for the units you are currently studying. Your tutor may have given you these, or you can find them in your course specification – go to www.edexcel.com.

b) Look at the grading grid for the units and identify the way the requirements change for the higher grades. If there are some unfamiliar words, check these in Step Six of this guide (see page 35 onwards).

c) If the unit points system still seems complicated, ask your tutor to explain it.

d) Check the UCAS points you would need for the course or university which interests you.

e) Design a form you can use to record the unit points you earn throughout your course. Keep this up to date. Regularly check how your points relate to your overall grade(s), based on the grade boundaries for your qualification. Your tutor can give you this information or you can check it yourself in the course specification.

Activity: Achieving UCAS points

Kera wants to go to university to do a degree in zoology, but the thought of doing exams to get in has put her off. Her careers advisor has recommended that she do a BTEC Level 3 National in Animal Care. This will provide her with all the knowledge about biology, anatomy and physiology needed to succeed at university without having to take exams. Plus there is the added bonus of being able to study at a centre that has a wide variety of animals, providing plenty of hands-on experience.

She has looked at prospectuses for different universities and she also knows the general level of UCAS points required for entry onto a zoology course. The question now is how to get there.

In the table below, list five things that Kera might do to plan her assessment load and achieve the required UCAS points.

1.	
2.	
3.	
4.	
5.	

Step Three: Understand yourself

Case study: What do you want to do?

Kate has loads of friends, but they are all interested in different things. Most of them are planning to do A-levels, but Kate isn't really interested in focusing on a small number of subjects. The problem is that although Kate is really good at many things, sitting in a classroom all day simply doesn't appeal to her. She wants to do something different, but doesn't know where to start.

One of her friends is planning to do a BTEC Level 3 National in Countryside Management. Kate looks at the variety of units on offer. There are some science ones, some units on wildlife habitats, countryside recreation and interpretation, even some units on countryside pursuits and greenwood crafts. Kate is a natural at science and is really keen on helping wildlife. She likes writing creatively and thinks that some of the countryside units will be fun to study.

Kate's Dad is not so sure. He thinks the qualification is not suitable for his bright

daughter but Kate assures him that it is exactly the right thing for her as a BTEC Level 3 National in Countryside Management is full of transferable skills. During the time that Kate is doing the qualification, she will be preparing for a career in the countryside. While Kate is deciding exactly what to do, she will be learning a range of science, writing and other skills that will put her in good stead to do almost whatever she wants. This could be another vocational qualification, or it could be university – but for now it is doing something that she knows she wants to do.

Reflection point

Do you like being outdoors? Do you want a career that lets you do what you like doing? If so, there's a BTEC National in the land and environment sector that is right for you. Which one is it?

Self-awareness means understanding how you 'tick'. For example, do you prefer practical activities rather than theory? Do you prefer to draw or sketch an idea, rather than write about it?

Self-awareness is important as it makes you less reliant on other people's opinions and gives you confidence in your own judgement as you reflect on your actions and learn from your experiences.

Self-awareness also means knowing your own strengths and weaknesses. Knowing your strengths enables you to feel positive and confident about yourself and your abilities. Knowing your weaknesses means you know the areas you need to develop.

You can analyse yourself by looking at...

... your personality and preferences

You may have taken a personality test at your centre. If not, your tutor may recommend one to use, or there are many available online.

Many employers ask job candidates to complete a personality test so that they can match the type of work they are offering to the most suitable people. Although these tests can only give a broad indication of someone's personality they may help to avoid mismatches, such as hiring someone who is introverted to work in sales.

... your skills and abilities

To succeed in your assignments, and to progress in a career, requires a number of skills. Some may be vocationally specific, or professional, skills that you can improve during your course – such as sporting performance on a Sports course. Others are broader skills that are invaluable no matter what you are studying – such as communicating clearly and co-operating with others.

You will work faster and more accurately, and have greater confidence, if you are skilled and proficient. A quick skills check will identify any problem areas.

TOP TIP

Use the Skills building section on page 85 to identify the skills you need for your course. You'll also find hints and tips for improving any weak areas.

Key points

- You need certain skills and abilities to get the most out of your BTEC Level 3 National course and to develop your career potential.
- Knowing your strengths and weaknesses is a sign of maturity. It gives you greater confidence in your abilities and enables you to focus on areas for improvement.

TOP TIP

You will find more help in this guide on developing your skills in using time wisely (Step Four), working as a member of a group (Step Seven), researching and analysing information (Step Eight) and making effective presentations (Step Nine).

Action points

1 Gain insight into your own personality by ticking **True** or **False** against each of the following statements. Be honest!

		True	False
a)	If someone annoys me, I can tell them about it without causing offence.		
b)	If someone is talking, I often interrupt them to give them my opinion.		
c)	I get really stressed if I'm under pressure.		
d)	I can sometimes become very emotional and upset on other people's behalf.		
e)	I sometimes worry that I can't cope and may make a mess of something.		
f)	I am usually keen, enthusiastic and motivated to do well.		
g)	I enjoy planning and organising my work.		
h)	I find it easy to work and co-operate with other people and take account of their opinions.		
i)	I am easily influenced by other people.		
j)	I often jump to conclusions and judge people and situations on first impressions.		
k)	I prefer to rely on facts and experience rather than following my instincts.		

Now identify which of the skills and qualities in the box below will be really important in your chosen career.

> tact   truthfulness   listening skills
>
> **staying calm under pressure**
>
> **empathy with others**   self-confidence
>
> initiative   planning and organising
>
> working with others   self-assurance
>
> objective judgements

Use your answers to identify areas you should work on to be successful in the future.

2   As part of the UCAS process, all **higher education** applicants have to write a personal statement. This is different from a CV, which is a summary of achievements that all job applicants prepare. You may have already prepared a CV but not thought about a personal statement. Now is your chance!

Read the information about personal statement in the box. Then answer these questions:

a)   Explain why personal statements are so important for higher education applicants.

b)   Why do you think it is important for your personal statement to read well and be error-free?

c)   Suggest three reasons why you shouldn't copy a pre-written statement you have found online.

d)   Check websites with information about personal statements to see what to include in the statement and how to set it out.

e)   Prepare a bullet point list of ten personal facts. Focus on your strengths and good reasons why you should be given a place on the higher education course of your choice. If possible, discuss your list with your tutor. Then keep it safe, as it will be useful if you need to write a personal statement later.

Personal statements

This is the information that all higher education applicants have to put in the blank space on their UCAS form. The aim is to sell yourself to admissions tutors. It can be pretty scary, especially if you haven't written anything like it before.

So, where do you start?

First, *never* copy pre-written statements you find online. These are just for guidance. Even worse are websites that offer to write your statement for a fee, and send you a few general, pre-written paragraphs. Forget them all: you can do better!

Imagine you are an admissions tutor with 60 places to offer to 200 applicants. What will you need to read in a personal statement to persuade you to offer the applicant a place?

Most likely, clear explanations about:

- what the applicant can contribute to the course

- why the applicant really wants a place on your course

- what the applicant has done to further his/her own interests in this area, such as voluntary work

- attributes that show this applicant would be a definite bonus – such as innovative ideas, with evidence eg 'I organised a newsletter which we published every three months …'

A personal statement should be well written, with no grammatical or spelling errors, and organised into clear paragraphs.

For further guidance on personal statements, go to page 96 to find out how to access a number of helpful websites.

Activity: Skills gained on a BTEC

Chris has just completed a BTEC Level 3 National in Horticulture. He worked hard on the course and did well. In addition, he had a good work placement at a local garden centre. He has noticed a job advert in the paper from another garden centre that is recruiting staff.

As part of his course, Chris has prepared a good, up-to-date and relevant CV. Now he needs to write a letter highlighting the reasons why he is the right person for the job. The BTEC National in Horticulture has equipped Chris with plenty of technical skills, so he stands a good chance of getting an interview. But there's more to a garden centre than just plants.

In the boxes below, set out four skills that Chris would have obtained from the course and his work experience that give him an advantage over other candidates.

1.	
2.	
3.	
4.	

Step Four: Use your time wisely

Case study: Work smart

Harry is a keen sportsman and plays rugby, cricket and hockey. With practice sessions and matches, combined with a part-time job, Harry has quite a tight schedule. He is also doing a BTEC Level 3 National in Forestry and Arboriculture, and has just been given an assignment that is due in three weeks. He already has two assignments to complete – one due next week and one the week after. That's three assignments in three weeks!

Harry is not bothered by the workload of assignments as he has a plan.

Harry attends the centre four days a week. However, on one day, there is a morning set aside for study. Harry uses this time to read the forestry journals, make notes and goes online to search the internet. He prints useful information and checks his emails. He deletes the junk and makes a few replies, but keeps an eye on the time. He also checks out a good book for the assignment due at the end of the third week. In addition to the morning study period, there is a chainsaw session and a tractor-driving session.

Both can only cater for part of the class, so every other week, Harry either goes home or stays and works in the library as it has a good computer and printing service, plus access to the forestry magazines and books.

Harry manages to complete the first assignment with three days to spare. When he prints his second one, the library printer breaks down, but he still has three days before it is due and is able to print it at lunchtime the following day. Despite the technical glitch, he has it ready with a day to spare. The third assignment is a report describing 10 commercial softwood trees. The book Harry had got out of the library has all the information he needs.

Harry's got his act together all right. But it's not because he's working hard; it's because he's working smart.

Reflection point

What can you do to work smart?

Most learners have to combine course commitments with other responsibilities such as a job (either full time or part-time) and family responsibilities. You will also want to see your friends and keep up your hobbies and interests. Juggling these successfully means you need to be able to use your time wisely.

This involves planning what to do and when to do it to prevent panics about unexpected deadlines. As your course progresses, this becomes even more important as your workload may increase towards the end of a term. In some cases, there could be two or more assignments to complete simultaneously. Although tutors try to avoid clashes of this sort, it is sometimes inevitable.

TOP TIPS

When researching for assignments produce a checklist of all the information you have to gather. It will help you to remain focused and on task.

To cope successfully, you need time-management skills, in particular:

- how to organise your time to be more productive
- how to prioritise tasks
- how to overcome time-wasters.

Organising your time

- **Use a diary or wall chart.**
  Using a different colour pen for each, enter:
  - your course commitments, such as assignment dates, tutorials, visits
  - important personal commitments, such as sports matches, family birthdays
  - your work commitments.

> **TOP TIP**
>
> A diary is useful because you can update it as you go, but a wall chart gives you a better overview of your commitments over several weeks. Keep your diary or chart up to date, and check ahead regularly so that you have prior warning of important dates.

- **Identify how you currently use your time.**
  - Work out how much time you spend at your centre, at work, at home and on social activities.
  - Identify which commitments are vital and which are optional, so you can find extra time if necessary.

- **Plan and schedule future commitments.**
  - Write down any appointments and tasks you must do.
  - Enter assignment review dates and final deadline dates in different colours.
  - This should stop you from arranging a dental appointment on the same morning that you are due to give an important presentation – or planning a hectic social life when you have lots of course work to do.

- **Decide your best times for doing course work.**
  - Expect to do most of your course work in your own time.
  - Work at the time of day when you feel at your best.
  - Work regularly, and in relatively short bursts, rather than once or twice a week for very long stretches.
  - If you're a night owl, allow an hour to 'switch off' before you go to bed.

- **Decide where to work.**
  - Choose somewhere you can concentrate without interruption.
  - Make sure there is space for resources you use, such as books or specialist equipment.
  - You also need good lighting and a good – but not too comfortable – chair.
  - If you can't find suitable space at home, check out your local or college library.

- **Assemble the items you need.**
  - Book ahead to get specific books, journals or DVDs from the library.
  - Ensure you have your notes, handouts and assignment brief with you.
  - Use sticky notes to mark important pages in textbooks or folders.

> **TOP TIP**
>
> Set yourself a target when you start work, so that you feel positive and productive at the end. Always try to end a session when a task is going well, rather than when you are stuck. Then you will be keener to go back to it the next day. Note down outstanding tasks you need to continue with next time.

- **Plan ahead.**
  - If anything is unclear about an assignment, ask your tutor for an explanation as soon as you can.
  - Break down assignments into manageable chunks, such as find information, decide what to use, create a plan for finished work, write rough draft of first section etc.
  - Work back from deadline dates so that you allow plenty of time to do the work.
  - Always allow more time than you need. It is better to finish early than to run out of time.

TOP TIP

If you are working on a task as a group, organise and agree times to work together. Make sure you have somewhere to meet where you can work without disturbing other courses or groups.

- **Be self-disciplined.**
  - Don't put things off because you're not in the mood. Make it easier by doing simple tasks first to get a sense of achievement. Then move on to something harder.
  - Plan regular breaks. If you're working hard, you need a change of activity to recharge your batteries.
  - If you have a serious problem or personal crisis, talk to your personal tutor promptly.

TOP TIP

Make sure you know the consequences of missing an assignment deadline, as well as the dispensations and exemptions that can be given if you have an unavoidable and serious problem, such as illness (see also page 83).

How to prioritise tasks

Prioritising means doing the most important and urgent task first. Normally this will be the task or assignment with the closest deadline or the one that will most affect your overall course grades.

One way of prioritising is to group tasks into ABC categories.

Category A tasks	These must be done now as they are very important and cannot be delayed, such as completing an assignment to be handed in tomorrow.
Category B tasks	These are jobs you should do if you have time, because otherwise they will rapidly become Category A, such as getting a book that you need for your next assignment.
Category C tasks	These are tasks you should do if you have the time, such as rewriting notes jotted down quickly in a lesson.

Expect to be flexible. For example, if you need to allow time for information to arrive, then send for this first. If you are working in a team, take into account other people's schedules when you are making arrangements.

Avoiding time-wasters

Everyone has days when they don't know where the time has gone. It may be because they were constantly interrupted or because things just kept going wrong. Whatever the reason, the end result is that some jobs don't get done.

If this happens to you regularly, you need to take steps to keep on track. Here are some useful tips.

- **Warn people in advance when you will be working.**
  - Ask them to not interrupt you.
  - If you are in a separate room, shut the door. If someone comes in, make it clear you don't want to talk.
  - If that doesn't work, find somewhere else (or some other time) to work.
- **Switch off your mobile, the television and radio, and your iPod/MP3 player.**
  - Don't respond to, or make, calls or texts.
  - If someone rings your home phone, let voicemail answer or ask them to call back later.
- **Be strict with yourself when you are working online.**
  - Don't check your email until you've finished work.
  - Don't get distracted when searching for information.
  - Keep away from social networking sites.
- **Avoid displacement activities.**
  - These are the normally tedious jobs, such as cleaning your computer screen, that suddenly seem far more attractive than working!

Talking to friends can occupy a lot of time.

> **TOP TIP**
>
> The first step in managing your own time is learning to say 'no' (nicely!) if someone asks you to do something tempting when you should be working.

Key points

- Being in control of your time allows you to balance your commitments according to their importance and means you won't let anyone down.
- Organising yourself and your time involves knowing how you spend your time now, planning when and where it is best to work, scheduling commitments and setting sensible timescales to complete your work.
- Knowing how to prioritise means you will schedule work effectively according to its urgency and importance. You will need self-discipline to follow the schedule you have set for yourself.
- Identifying ways in which you may waste time means you can guard against these to achieve your goals more easily.

> **TOP TIP**
>
> Benefits to managing your own time include being less stressed (because you are not reacting to problems or crises), producing better work and having time for a social life.

Action points

1 Start planning your time properly.

a) Find out how many assignments you will have this term, and when you will get them. Put this information into your diary or planner.

b) Update this with your other commitments for the term – both work/course-related and social. Identify possible clashes and decide how to resolve the problem.

c) Identify one major task or assignment you will do soon. Divide it into manageable chunks and decide how long to allow for each chunk, plus some spare time for any problems. If possible, check your ideas with your tutor before you put them into your planner.

2 How good are you at being responsible for your own learning?

a) Fill in this table. Score yourself out of 5 for each area: where 0 is awful and 5 is excellent. Ask a friend or relative to score you as well. See if you can explain any differences.

	Scoring yourself	Other person's score for you
Being punctual		
Organisational ability		
Tidiness		
Working accurately		
Finding and correcting own mistakes		
Solving problems		
Accepting responsibility		
Working with details		
Planning how to do a job		
Using own initiative		
Thinking up new ideas		
Meeting deadlines		

b) Draw up your own action plan for areas where you need to improve. If possible, talk this through at your next **tutorial** (see page 100).

TOP TIP

Don't waste time doing things that distract you when studying for this course. In a travel business, time costs money.

Activity: Responding to interview questions

Laksmi has completed a BTEC Level 3 National in Floristry and is applying to become the assistant manager at the florist where she is currently doing her work-based learning. Although the manager has suggested that Laksmi apply for the job, she still has to go through the interview process.

At the interview, the manager sets Laksmi four scenarios. How might Laksmi respond?

Scenario	Response
As you are serving a customer, the phone rings. What would you do next?	
You are making a delivery and the recipient is so excited to receive the flowers from her boyfriend that she invites you in for a cup of tea. What would you do?	
A colleague has just broken up with his boyfriend and is telling you about it on your mobile when a customer walks in. What would you do?	
It's 11.30am and you are halfway through a large order of three bouquets that have to be completed by the end of the day when a customer walks in and places an order for a corsage to pick up in an hour's time. How would you prioritise your work?	

Step Five: Utilise all your resources

Case study: Researching an assignment

Steve is studying for a BTEC Level 3 National in Agriculture, and for his current assignment he needs to design a milking parlour for a local dairy. This is quite an important assignment, and he needs a distinction to get enough UCAS points for his university course. He does a quick search on the internet, but all he can find is information from a website in the USA. That provides some useful information, but Steve is not sure if some of the information, such as the minimum legal requirements stated on the website, applies to the UK.

Steve goes into the library and finds a good textbook describing several designs of milking parlours. He also gets some information from one of the magazines in the library that specialises in dairy production.

Now Steve has plenty of information, but as he sits down to put it all together, he is a bit confused. He has plenty of design ideas, but he can't decide which is the best one to include in his assignment. He goes back to the library, and the librarian helps him to find an agricultural journal that contains some good research on evaluating dairy systems.

Despite having the extra information, Steve still finds that he needs more direction. He mentions this to his tutor, who gives him a couple of contacts at two local dairy farms. He follows up the contacts and they give him some very useful information. He now has everything he needs to complete his assignment.

Through this process, Steve has learned a couple of important points:

1 You don't always find everything you need for an assignment from one source.

2 Sometimes, not all the information you need is in print or on the internet: you can also get some really useful information by talking to people in the industry.

Reflection points

Can you see the advantages of using more than one source?

Your resources are all the things that can help you to be successful in your BTEC Level 3 National qualification, from your favourite website to your **study buddy** (see page 32) who collects handouts for you if you miss a class.

Your centre will provide essential resources, such as a library with appropriate books and electronic reference sources, the computer network and internet access. You will have to provide basic resources such as pens, pencils and file folders yourself. If you have to buy your own textbooks, look after them carefully so you can sell them on at the end of your course.

Here is a list of resources, with tips for getting the best out of them.

- **Course information**. This includes your course specification, this Study Skills Guide and all information on the Edexcel website relating to your BTEC Level 3 National course. Course information from your centre will include term dates, assignment dates and your timetable. Keep everything safely so you can refer to it whenever you need to clarify something.

- **Course materials**. These include course handouts, printouts, your own notes and textbooks. Put handouts into an A4 folder as soon as you get them. Use a separate folder for each unit you study.

> **TOP TIP**
>
> Filing notes and handouts promptly means they don't get lost, and will stay clean and uncrumpled, and you won't waste time looking for them.

- **Stationery**. You need pens and pencils, a notepad, a hole puncher, a stapler and sets of dividers. Dividers should be clearly labelled to help you store and quickly find notes, printouts and handouts. Your notes should be headed and dated, and those from your own research must also include your source (see Step Eight, page 63 onwards.)

- **People**. Your tutors, specialist staff at college, classmates, your employer and work colleagues, your relatives and friends are all valuable resources. Many will have particular skills or work in the vocational area that you are studying. Talking to other learners can help to clarify issues that there may not have been time to discuss fully in class.

A **study buddy** is another useful resource as they can make notes and collect handouts if you miss a session. (Remember to return the favour when they are away.)

Always be polite when you are asking people for information. Prepare the questions first and remember that you are asking for help, not trying to get them to do the work for you! If you are interviewing someone for an assignment or project, good preparations are vital. (See Step Eight, page 63 onwards.)

If someone who did the course before you offers help, be careful. It is likely the course requirements will have changed. Never be tempted to copy their assignments (or someone else's). This is **plagiarism** – a deadly sin in the educational world (see also Step Six, page 35.)

> **TOP TIP**
>
> A positive attitude, an enquiring mind and the ability to focus on what is important will have a major impact on your final result.

Key points

- Resources help you to achieve your qualification. Find out what resources you have available to you and use them wisely.

- Have your own stationery items.

- Know how to use central facilities and resources such as the library, learning resource centres and your computer network. Always keep to the policy on IT use in your centre.

- People are a key resource – school or college staff, work colleagues, members of your class, friends, family and people who are experts in their field.

Action points

1 a) List the resources you will need to complete your course successfully. Identify which ones will be provided by your school or college, and which you need to supply yourself.

b) Go through your list again and identify the resources you already have (or know how to access) and those you don't.

c) Compare your list with a friend's and decide how to obtain and access the resources you need. Add any items to your list that you forgot.

d) List the items you still need to get and set a target date for doing this.

2 'Study buddy' schemes operate in many centres. Find out if this applies to your own centre and how you can make the best use of it.

In some you can choose your study buddy, in others people are paired up by their tutor.

- Being a study buddy might mean just collecting handouts when the other person is absent, and giving them important news.

- It may also mean studying together and meeting (or keeping contact by phone or email) to exchange ideas and share resources.

With a study buddy you can share resources and stay on top of the course if you're ever away.

Activity: Resources

Ross is struggling to complete his assignment on canine anatomy and physiology. The assignment requires learners to illustrate the different organs and explain how they work. Ross is okay with that part, but he is stumped on the merit task that asks learners to compare the anatomy and physiology systems of cats and dogs. He has a handout and the notes that he took from the lecture, but he doesn't really understand them.

Ross talks to his tutor, who clarifies the assignment requirements and points out some useful sources. His tutor says that there is a very good textbook available in the library and mentions some very useful posters on the wall in the classroom, which Ross can study during his break. He also reminds Ross about the 3-D models of animals in the laboratory that could be useful for helping Ross to visualise the concepts.

In the table below, identify some other resources that Ross could use to help him complete his assignment.

1.	
2.	
3	
4.	

Step Six: Understand your assessment

Case study: Covering the grading criteria

Amy has been given an assignment as part of her BTEC Level 3 National in Forestry. It has two pass criteria and one merit criterion. All the criteria are linked in some way. For example, one pass criterion requires learners to explain techniques and practices to protect forests and woodlands from fire, while the other one asks learners to evaluate techniques and practices to protect forests and woodlands from pests. The connection is very clear, as both criteria relate to protecting forests. The merit criterion – recommend suitable protection methods for a newly-planted woodland on a given site – also involves forest protection.

The assignment brief requires evidence to be produced for each criterion as an oral presentation. Amy ponders whether this means one presentation for all of them, or two presentations (one for the pass criteria and one for the merit criterion), or three presentations (one for each of the criteria)?

BTEC assignments lay out the criteria clearly (you always know what you have to do to get a pass, merit or distinction). To complete the assignment, all that Amy has to do is one presentation that covers all three criteria. However, to ensure that it is clear to the tutor, Amy should highlight the three criteria during the presentation.

Reflection points

How might you create a presentation that covers all three criteria?

Being successful on any BTEC Level 3 National course means first understanding what you must do in your assignments – and then doing it.

Your assignments focus on topics you have already covered in class. If you've attended regularly, you should be able to complete them confidently.

However, there are some common pitfalls it's worth thinking about. Here are tips to avoid them:

- Read the instructions (the assignment brief) properly and several times before you start.
- Make sure you understand what you are supposed to do. Ask if anything is unclear.

- Complete every part of a task. If you ignore a question, you can't meet the grading criteria.
- Prepare properly. Do your research or reading before you start. Don't guess the answers.
- Communicate your ideas clearly. You can check this by asking someone who doesn't know the subject to look at your work.
- Only include relevant information. Padding out answers makes it look as if you don't know your subject.
- Do the work earlier rather than later to avoid any last-minute panics.
- Pay attention to advice and feedback that your tutor has given you.

The assignment 'brief'

This may be longer than its name implies! The assignment brief includes all the instructions for an assignment and several other details, as you can see in the table below.

What will you find in a BTEC Level 3 National assignment brief?	
Content	**Details**
Title	This will link to the unit and learning outcomes
Format/style	Written assignment, presentation, demonstration, etc
Preparation	Read case study, do research, etc
Learning outcomes	These state the knowledge you must demonstrate to obtain a required grade
Grading criterion/ criteria covered	Fo example, P1, M1, D1
Individual/group work	Remember to identify your own contribution in any group work
Feedback	Tutor, peer review
Interim review dates	Dates to see your tutor
Final deadline	Last submission date

Your centre's rules and regulations

Your centre will have several policies and guidelines about assignments, which you need to check carefully. Many, such as those listed below, relate to Edexcel policies and guidelines.

- The procedure to follow if you have a serious problem and can't meet a deadline. An extension may be granted.
- The penalty for missing a deadline without good reason.
- The penalty for copying someone else's work. This is usually severe, so never share your work (or CDs or USB flash drive) with anyone else, and don't borrow theirs.
- **Plagiarism** is also serious misconduct. This means copying someone's work or quoting from books and websites and pretending it is your own work.
- The procedure to follow if you disagree with the grade you are given.

Understanding the question or task

There are two aspects to a question or task. The first is the **command words**, which are described below. The second is the **presentation instructions**, which is what you are asked to do – don't write a report when you should be producing a chart!

Command words, such as 'explain', 'describe', 'analyse', 'evaluate' state how a question must be answered. You may be asked to 'describe' something at pass level, but you will need to do more, perhaps 'analyse' or 'evaluate', to achieve merit or distinction.

Many learners fail to achieve higher grades because they don't realise the difference between these words. Instead of analysing or evaluating they give an explanation instead. Adding more details won't achieve a higher grade – you need to change your whole approach to the answer.

The **grading grid** for each unit of your course gives you the command words, so that you know what to do to achieve a pass, merit or distinction. The tables that follow show you what is usually required when you see a particular command word. These are just examples to guide you as the exact response will depend on the question. If you have any doubts, check with your tutor before you start work.

There are two important points to note.

- A command word, such as 'create' or 'explain' may be repeated in the grading criteria for different grades. In these cases the complexity or range of the task itself increases at the higher grades.

- Command words vary depending on your vocational area. So Art and Design grading grids may use different command words from Applied Science, for example.

TOP TIP

Look at this section again when you get your first assignment and check the command words against these explanations.

To obtain a pass grade

To achieve a pass you must usually demonstrate that you understand the important facts relating to a topic and can state these clearly and concisely.

Command words for a pass	Meaning
Create (or produce)	Make, invent or construct an item.
Describe	Give a clear, straightforward description that includes all the main points and links these together logically.
Define	Clearly explain what a particular term means and give an example, if appropriate, to show what you mean.
Explain … how/why	Set out in detail the meaning of something, with reasons. It is often helpful to give an example of what you mean. Start with the topic then give the 'how' or 'why'.
Identify	Distinguish and state the main features or basic facts relating to a topic.
Interpret	Define or explain the meaning of something.
Illustrate	Give examples to show what you mean.
List	Provide the information required in a list rather than in continuous writing.
Outline	Write a clear description that includes all the main points but avoid going into too much detail.
Plan (or devise)	Work out and explain how you would carry out a task or activity.
Select (and present) information	Identify relevant information to support the argument you are making and communicate this in an appropriate way.
State	Write a clear and full account.
Undertake	Carry out a specific activity.
Examples:	
Identify the main features on a digital camera.	
Outline the steps to take to carry out research for an assignment.	

To obtain a merit grade

To obtain a merit you must prove that you can apply your knowledge in a specific way.

Command words for a merit	Meaning
Analyse	Identify separate factors, say how they relate to each other and how each one relates to the topic.
Classify	Sort your information into appropriate categories before presenting or explaining it.
Compare and contrast	Identify the main factors that apply in two or more situations and explain the similarities and differences or advantages and disadvantages.
Demonstrate	Provide several relevant examples or appropriate evidence which support the arguments you are making. In some vocational areas this may also mean giving a practical performance.
Discuss	Provide a thoughtful and logical argument to support the case you are making.
Explain (in detail)	Provide details and give reasons and/or evidence to clearly support the argument you are making.
Implement	Put into practice or operation. You may also have to interpret or justify the effect or result.
Interpret	Understand and explain an effect or result.
Justify	Give appropriate reasons to support your opinion or views and show how you arrived at these conclusions.
Relate/report	Give a full account, with reasons.
Research	Carry out a full investigation.
Specify	Provide full details and descriptions of selected items or activities.
Examples:	
Compare and contrast the performance of two different digital cameras.	
Explain in detail the steps to take to research an assignment.	

To obtain a distinction grade

To obtain a distinction you must prove that you can make a reasoned judgement based on appropriate evidence.

Command words for a distinction	Meaning
Analyse	Identify the key factors, show how they are linked and explain the importance and relevance of each.
Assess	Give careful consideration to all the factors or events that apply and identify which are the most important and relevant, with reasons.
Comprehensively explain	Give a very detailed explanation that covers all the relevant points and give reasons for your views or actions.
Critically comment	Give your view after you have considered all the evidence, particularly the importance of both the relevant positive and negative aspects.
Evaluate	Review the information and then bring it together to form a conclusion. Give evidence to support each of your views or statements.
Evaluate critically	Review the information to decide the degree to which something is true, important or valuable. Then assess possible alternatives, taking into account their strengths and weaknesses if they were applied instead. Then give a precise and detailed account to explain your opinion.
Summarise	Identify/review the main, relevant factors and/or arguments so that these are explained in a clear and concise manner.
Examples:	
Assess ten features commonly found on a digital camera.	
Analyse your own ability to carry out effective research for an assignment.	

TOP TIP

Check that you understand exactly how you need to demonstrate each of the learning outcomes specified in the assignment.

Responding positively

Assignments enable you to demonstrate what you know and how you can apply it. You should respond positively to the challenge and give it your best shot. Being well organised and having confidence in your own abilities helps too, and this is covered in the next section.

Key points

- Read instructions carefully so that you don't make mistakes that can easily be avoided, such as only doing part of the set task.
- Note the assignment deadline on your planner and any interim review dates. Schedule work around these dates to make the most of reviews with your tutor.
- Check your centre's policies relating to assignments, such as how to obtain an extension or query a final grade.
- Expect command words and/or the complexity of a task to be different at higher grades, because you have to demonstrate higher-level skills.

TOP TIP

All your assignments will relate to topics you have covered and work you have done in class. They're not meant to be a test to catch you out.

Action points

1 Check your ability to differentiate between different types of command words by doing this activity.
   a) Prepare a brief description of your usual lifestyle (pass level).
   b) Describe and justify your current lifestyle (merit level).
   c) Critically evaluate your current lifestyle (distinction level).

It would be a good idea to check that your answer is accurate and appropriate by showing it to your tutor at your next tutorial.

TOP TIP

When presenting evidence for an assessment, think about the person who will be looking through it. Plan your 'pitch' well and make it easy for the assessor to match your evidence against the grading criteria.

Sample assignment

Front sheet

Read the assignment front sheet through carefully and check that your work links to the criteria covered by this assignment.

Refer to your school or college's policy on late submissions. If in doubt, ask your tutor.

If you are unsure if your work meets the grading criteria, ask your tutor to review it a few days before submission.

Pay close attention to the information in the task descriptions to ensure that the work you produce meets the grading criteria and that you provide the evidence that has been requested.

Learner name		Assessor name	
Jane Doe		Mrs Tamsin Lockthwaite	
Date issued	Completion date		Submitted on
20 May 2011	24 June 2011		22 June 2011
Qualification		Unit	
BTEC Level 3 Diploma in Countryside Management		Unit 31: Understanding Woodland Management	

Assignment title	Management Planning

In this assignment you will have opportunities to provide evidence against the following criteria.
Indicate the page numbers where the evidence can be found.

Criteria reference	To achieve the criteria the evidence must show that the student is able to:	Task no.	Evidence
P8	Explain the structure, content and presentation of a woodland management plan	1	1–5 Observation record
P9	Explain how to achieve the best balance between present and potential woodland uses covering: i) legal ii) environmental iii) requirements of woodland users iv) economic/financial v) physical	2	6–8
P10	Explain techniques used to assess woodlands	1	1–5
M4	Assess the suitability of a woodland for given activities	2	6–8
D2	Evaluate a selected management plan and suggest improvements	3	9

Learner declaration
I certify that the work submitted for this assignment is my own and research sources are fully acknowledged. Learner signature: Jane Doe   Date: 22 June 2011

This table shows how each task is linked to the grading criteria and the location of the appropriate evidence in your work.

Provide proper references for your work, including a list of your sources at the end of each task. Do not cut and paste information from websites or copy the work of other learners.

Assignment brief

The scenario helps to set the scene for your assignment. You should take some time to consider the scenario. For example, a woodland officer would be expected to have a good understanding of the management planning process and be able to assess woodlands, explain management techniques, and discuss constraints and opportunities.

Always keep the assignment title in mind to help you focus your work.

Practice your presentation several times to ensure that you can get across the required information within the 10 minute time limit.

Qualification	BTEC Level 3 Diploma in Countryside Management
Unit title	Unit 31: Understanding Woodland Management
Start date	20 May 2011
Deadline date	24 June 2011
Assessor	Mrs Tamsin Lockthwaite

Assignment title	Management Planning

The purpose of this assignment is to enable you to gain an understanding of the structure and content of a woodland management plan and its importance for guiding management activities.

Scenario

As a tree and woodland officer for a local council, you have been asked to attend a meeting of the Environment Committee. You have asked for funding to write a management plan for a popular woodland site owned by the council. You have been called to the meeting to explain to officers what a management plan is and why you need one.

Task 1

a) Prepare a ten minute presentation on woodland management planning that explains the structure, content and presentation of a woodland management plan. Include in your presentation the importance of:
  • a site description
  • prescriptions (recommendations)
  • action plans and budgets.

Also explain the types of information that will have to be gathered, including sources, such as Ordnance Survey maps, soil/geology maps, mensuration surveys, ecology/habitat surveys, historical records. (**P8**)

b) As part of your presentation, explain the techniques used to assess woodlands for different purposes, such as estimating the timber resource, monitoring pests and diseases, determining landscape value and recording wildlife habitats. (**P10**)

Evidence required: oral presentation with accompanying notes

This provides evidence for P8, P10

Task 2

You have been given permission by the Environment Committee to produce a leaflet to provide an explanation on how to achieve the best balance between present and potential uses of the popular, local woodland site for which you wish to write a management plan. The leaflet will be used to call on views from the public on how they would like their site to be used. To prepare your research for the leaflet you will need to visit the woodland. Your research should cover the following four factors (**P9**):

a) Legal and Environmental Considerations: explain the constraints that could be imposed by felling licences, tree preservation orders, EU Species Directive 1992, Site of Special Scientific Interest (SSSI) and Area of Outstanding Natural Beauty (AONB), Local Nature Reserve (LNR).

b) Economic and Financial Considerations: identify possible sources of income, such as government grants, sales of products and limitations imposed by access to markets.

c) Requirements of Woodland Users: explain the current and potential uses of the woodland for walking, exercising dogs, picnics and the provision of suitable facilities, taking into account proximity to a population centre and public attitudes.

d) Physical Limitations: explain factors such as access to and within the site, exposure, site stability, soil drainage and potential effects of weather extremes such as drought, floods and winds.

As part of your leaflet provide an assessment of the woodland for use by the general public, including activities such as walking, exercising dogs and enjoying picnics. (**M4**)

Evidence required: illustrated leaflet

This provides evidence for P9, M4

Note that the evidence required is an illustrated leaflet. Make sure that you use photographs to highlight key points.

This presentation covers two grading criteria. Make sure that you clearly identify the evidence presented for each criterion.

A written report is required for this task – a couple a paragraphs will not be a sufficient response. If you are unsure what is needed, ask your tutor.

Textbooks will provide most of the information you need, and journals and websites will have good case studies.

Task 3

In the course of your work for the council, you discover in the archives a woodland management plan for another nearby woodland. Using information obtained from other sources, write a critique of the plan, including comments on how clear the plan is, its layout and structure, any missing information and make recommendations for improvements.

Evidence required: written report

This provides evidence for D2

Sources of information

Textbooks

Broad, K – *Caring for small woods: a practical manual for woodland owners, woodland managers, woodland craftsmen, foresters, land agents, project officers, conservationists, teachers and students* (Earthscan, 1998) ISBN 9781853834547

BTCV and Agate, E – *Woodlands: a practical handbook* (BTCV Enterprises, 2002) ISBN 9780946752331

Buckley, G P – *Ecology and management of coppice woodlands* (Chapman & Hall, 1992) ISBN 9780412431104

Fuller, R J – *Coppiced Woodlands: Their management for wildlife* (Joint Nature Conservation Committee, 1993) ISBN 9781873701324

Harmer, R and Howe, J – *The silviculture and management of coppice woodlands* (Forestry Commission, 2003) ISBN 085538591X

Hart, C – *Alternative silvicultural systems to clear cutting in Britain: a review* (Forestry Commission, 1995) ISBN 9780117103344

Hart, C – *Practical Forestry for the Agent and Surveyor* (Alan Sutton, 1991) ISBN 9780862999629

JNCC – *Field guide to woodland* (Joint Nature Conservation Committee, 2004) ISBN 9781861075239

Mackie, E and Matthews, R – *Timber measurement* (Forestry Commission, 2008) ISBN 9780855387495

Matthews, R W and Mackie, E D – *Forest mensuration: a handbook for practitioners* (Forestry Commission, 2006) ISBN 0855386215

Peterken, G F   *Woodland conservation and management* (Chapman & Hall, 1993) ISBN 9780412557309

Rackham, O – *Ancient Woodland; its history, vegetation and uses in England* (Nottingham University Press, 2003) ISBN 9781897604274

Starr, C – *Woodland management – a practical guide* (Crowood, 2005) ISBN 9781861267894

Journals

British Wildlife
Quarterly Journal of Forestry
Small Woods

Websites

British Trust for Conservation Volunteers **www.btcv.org.uk**
Forestry Commission **www.forestry.gov.uk**
Royal Forestry Association **www.rfs.org.uk**
Small Woods Association **www.smallwoods.org.uk**
Woodland Trust **www.woodlandtrust.org.uk**

This brief has beeen verified as being fit for purpose			
Assessor	Mrs Tamsin Lockthwaite		
Signature	*Tamsin Lockthwaite*	Date	*13 May 2011*
Internal verifier	Mr I Worrell		
Signature	*Ian Worrell*	Date	*13 May 2011*

Sample learner work

Note that the presenter has started by introducing herself as well as explaining the purpose of the presentation.

The presenter has created a graphic to illustrate the cyclical nature of woodland management planning.

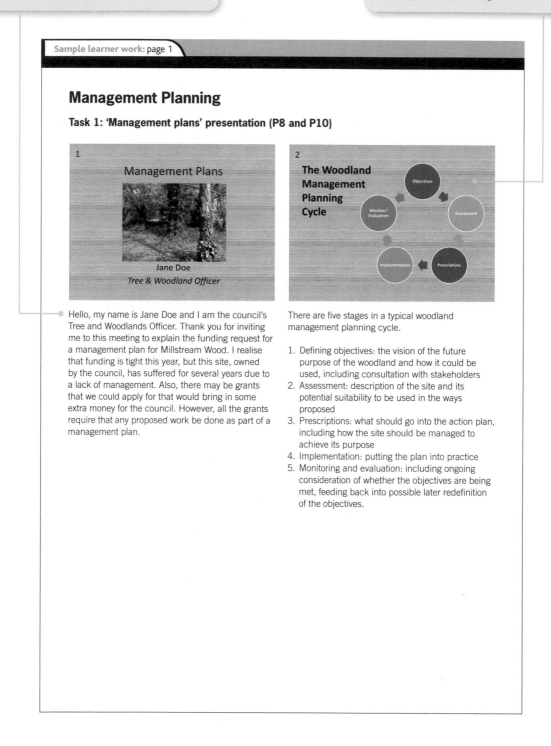

Sample learner work: page 1

Management Planning

Task 1: 'Management plans' presentation (P8 and P10)

1

Management Plans

Jane Doe
Tree & Woodland Officer

2

The Woodland Management Planning Cycle

Objectives
Assessment
Prescriptions
Implementation
Monitor/Evaluation

Hello, my name is Jane Doe and I am the council's Tree and Woodlands Officer. Thank you for inviting me to this meeting to explain the funding request for a management plan for Millstream Wood. I realise that funding is tight this year, but this site, owned by the council, has suffered for several years due to a lack of management. Also, there may be grants that we could apply for that would bring in some extra money for the council. However, all the grants require that any proposed work be done as part of a management plan.

There are five stages in a typical woodland management planning cycle.

1. Defining objectives: the vision of the future purpose of the woodland and how it could be used, including consultation with stakeholders
2. Assessment: description of the site and its potential suitability to be used in the ways proposed
3. Prescriptions: what should go into the action plan, including how the site should be managed to achieve its purpose
4. Implementation: putting the plan into practice
5. Monitoring and evaluation: including ongoing consideration of whether the objectives are being met, feeding back into possible later redefinition of the objectives.

Slides are kept to the point, with short informative statements. Most of the content is in the notes.

In addition to covering some specific material, this slide also provides an introduction to the next one.

Sample learner work: page 2

3 Woodland Aim/Objectives

- Aim: the 'big picture' – our long-term vision for the wood
- Objectives: how we will meet our aim
  - Starting point
  - Public consultation

Before we can make any work plans, we have to know what the vision for the wood is. I have some ideas, but this is a public open space, so the community should really have a say.

4 Assessment

- **Site description:** location, physical and biological features
- **Techniques and sources of information:** Ordnance Survey maps, soil and geology maps, mensuration surveys, ecological survey, historical records

The next part of the cycle is a description of the site. The community may have some big ideas, but they need to be considered in the light of the limitations of the site, particularly the physical features such as soils, drainage, access and size. In addition, surveys will need to be carried out to determine what plants and animals live there. If there are any rare ones, we will have to plan for their protection. We do have some survey records, but they are quite old and the information needs to be updated.

Required terms are explained within the context of the site being described.

As you write about a particular term (such as soil map), mark it on the task description. This makes it easier to track your progress.

Sample learner work: page 3

5 **Assessment:** Techniques and sources of information
- Ordnance Survey maps
- Soil and geology maps

Assessment techniques
- Timber resource assessment
  - Mensuration survey
  - Pests and diseases survey
- Woodland assessment for nature conservation
  - Ecology/habitat survey
- Landscape and cultural assessment
  - Historical records

Information from an OS map shows the size of the site and also provides a grid reference that pinpoints the location of the site. It also shows the contours and the altitude of the site.

Soil maps provide information on the soil types. Information from the UK Soil Survey provides descriptions of these soil types and their uses. Geology maps provide a picture of the underlying geology. Both these types of maps can usually be found in a local library.

Mensuration refers to woodland measurement. These surveys tell us how much timber there is (ie its volume in cubic metres) and the species, as well as giving an idea of the age distribution of the woodland. Several different techniques are used. These are generally called tariffing. They involve estimating the volume of a wood by measuring individual trees in plots and getting an average height and diameter. The Forestry Commission have tables that can be used to determine the timber volumes from this information. This is important because the wood is owned by the public and any economic value in the wood should be put to public use. For example, if we could sell some trees, we could use the money to put in some benches. Or there might be some other use for the trees. For example, the local green group is talking about renewable energy. There might be enough timber in the wood to run a wood fired power plant, but we won't know the answer to any of these possibilities unless a survey is done.

Additional information is also gathered in terms of the quality of the timber resource. This tends to be through making regular observations while going through the wood and doing the tree measurements. This is often affected by the presence of pests and diseases. One of the main local pests is the grey squirrel; however, squirrels are really popular with the public, so there may not be much we can do about it. However, if they are killing the trees, we might have to do something. We won't know unless a thorough survey is done.

The ecological survey will tell us what species live in the wood, as well as providing an estimate of the presence and estimated populations of any rare species that may be living there. It will also tell us about any interesting features, such as ancient trees or old hedgerows, which provide an idea of the history of the site. The trees and shrubs are identified and counted in large plots (often 100 m^2), while the plants are usually counted in 2 m quadrants. Insects are often gathered using sweep nets. Birds are generally recorded by observation or listening to bird song. Mammals are rarely seen, so evidence is gathered from the presence of tracks or burrows, such as badger setts.

The county museum or the county records centre or local history centre will probably have some information on the history of the wood. This, along with some of the biological information, could tell us if it is an ancient woodland. Ancient woodlands are very special places because there are not many of them about.

The OS maps will give us some idea of the importance of the site for local landscape value. However, the best way to do this is to gather photographic evidence of the wood from different local vantage points, such as from the top of Backbreak Hill, with photos taken at different times of the year. This will provide an idea of how important the woodland is for the landscape and could have an impact on any work that may be planned.

Although the two grading criteria have been well integrated, it would still be useful to have the evidence for P10 identified in the notes.

Sample learner work: page 4

6 Prescriptions

- Recommendations for management
- Provides the information for the Action Plan

Bearing in mind what people want from the site and its potential as identified in the site description, the consultants will come up with some recommendations for managing the site. These will form the basis of an Action Plan, which will then be reviewed and updated every year. This will help us to plan our work and make up budgets.

7 Implementation

- Carrying out the plan
- Working to an annual Action Plan

Once the plan has been completed, we will actually be able to do some work! If the community are interested, we may be able to form a 'Friends Group'. These are helpful in providing 'eyes and ears' on the site. Some groups actually do fundraising and carry out some of the management work, so they can be really useful.

Provide a complete list of your sources, including the authors, date, title and publisher of printed works, and the title and address of each website consulted.

Ensure that you finish a presentation with a clear conclusion that summarises your talk and stimulates discussion.

Sample learner work: page 5

8
Monitoring and evaluation

- Monitoring: More surveys!
- Evaluation
  - Checking progress
  - Modifications to prescriptions

9
Conclusion

- Management planning is a cycle
- Management plan is required for:
  - Meeting public expectations
  - Planning work
  - Evaluating progress
  - Obtaining funds

The purpose of monitoring is to make sure that everything is going to plan. We don't have any of our own countryside management staff to do this, so as part of our contract tender, we will ask the consultants to conduct a monitoring visit after Year 3 to see if our work is showing any results.

Depending on what the results of the monitoring are, we may have to evaluate our progress and revisit some of the management recommendations and make some modifications.

As you can see, a management plan is vital if we are going to effectively use the Millstream Wood site.

I hope you have found my presentation useful. Thank you for listening.

Any questions?

Bibliography

Alexander, M – *Management Planning for Nature Conservation* (Springer, 2007) ISBN 978-1402065804
BTCV and Agate, E - *Woodlands: a practical handbook* (BTCV Enterprises, 2002) ISBN 0946752338
Forestry Commission – *Management Plans for Semi-Natural Woodlands Under WGS* (Forestry Commission, 2009)
Lane, A and Tait, J – *Practical Conservation: Woodlands* (Open University, 1990) ISBN C1021

Observation record

Learner name	Jane Doe
Qualification	BTEC Level 3 Diploma in Countryside Management
Unit number and title	Unit 31: Understanding Woodland Management
Assignment title	Management Planning

Description of activity undertaken (please be as specific as possible)

This was a presentation with supporting notes designed to be delivered on the structure and content of a woodland management plan (**P8**) and the techniques used to assess woodlands (**P10**).

Assessment and grading criteria

P8: Explain the structure, content and presentation of a woodland management plan.

P10: Explain techniques used to assess woodlands.

How the activity meets the requirements of the assessment and grading criteria

Task 1
For **P8**, the learner provided a thorough explanation of the content, structure and presentation of a woodland management plan to an audience of peers. There was a good flow to the presentation and the content, as outlined in the unit description, was satisfactorily covered.

For **P10** the learner presented the information required integrated within the presentation for P8. A good explanation was provided of the different types of assessment involved for woodlands.

Assessor signature	*Tamsin Lockthwaite*	Date	*20 June 2011*
Assessor name	Mrs Tamsin Lockthwaite		

The first page indicates the purpose of the leaflet, which is described in the task description.

Illustrations are used throughout the leaflet to break up the text and highlight key points.

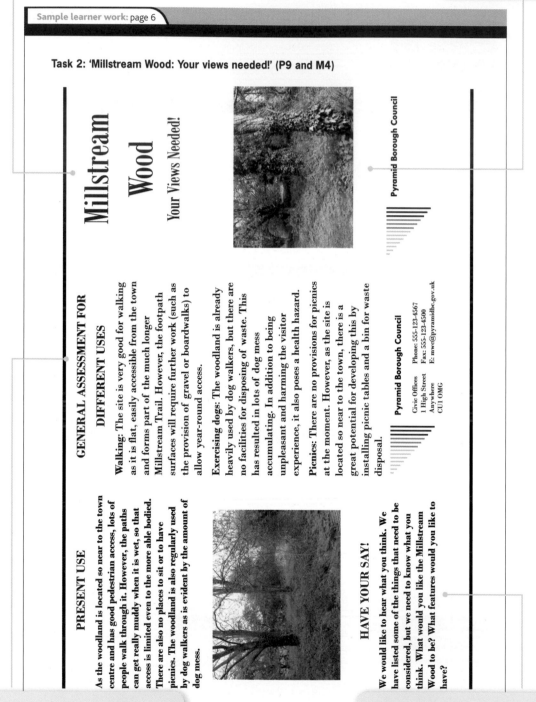

Sample learner work: page 6

Task 2: 'Millstream Wood: Your views needed!' (P9 and M4)

Millstream Wood
Your Views Needed!

Pyramid Borough Council

GENERAL ASSESSMENT FOR DIFFERENT USES

Walking: The site is very good for walking as it is flat, easily accessible from the town and forms part of the much longer Millstream Trail. However, the footpath surfaces will require further work (such as the provision of gravel or boardwalks) to allow year-round access.

Exercising dogs: The woodland is already heavily used by dog walkers, but there are no facilities for disposing of waste. This has resulted in lots of dog mess accumulating. In addition to being unpleasant and harming the visitor experience, it also poses a health hazard.

Picnics: There are no provisions for picnics at the moment. However, as the site is located so near to the town, there is a great potential for developing this by installing picnic tables and a bin for waste disposal.

Pyramid Borough Council

Civic Offices   Phone: 555-123-4567
1 High Street   Fax: 555-123-4500
Anywhere   E: mw@pyramidbc-gov.uk
CU1 OMG

PRESENT USE

As the woodland is located so near to the town centre and has good pedestrian access, lots of people walk through it. However, the paths can get really muddy when it is wet, so that access is limited even to the more able bodied. There are also no places to sit or to have picnics. The woodland is also regularly used by dog walkers as is evident by the amount of dog mess.

HAVE YOUR SAY!

We would like to hear what you think. We have listed some of the things that need to be considered, but we need to know what you think. What would you like the Millstream Wood to be? What features would you like to have?

The text is presented in small blocks separated by headings and sub-headings that correspond to the task description.

As the purpose of the leaflet is to obtain comments, different (fictional) contact methods have been provided.

Photographs have been used to highlight key points or provide a relevant local context to the leaflet.

MANAGEMENT CONSIDERATIONS

As part of the management plan process there are several factors to consider.

This leaflet will provide a general assessment of the woodland for use by the general public, dog walkers and picnickers, and explore how the following factors could influence decisions regarding the management of Millstream Wood:

- legal and environmental
- requirements of woodland users
- economic/financial
- physical

PHYSICAL FACTORS

Physical factors include location, soils, slope, size and aspect. Millstream Wood is located next to the millstream going through the town. It is well connected with tarmac paths leading from the town centre along the millstream. Thus, pedestrian access to the wood is very good.

It is a small wood (about one hectare), so the amount of activities it can hold is very limited. Also, it is a low lying flat site with moderate exposure, which is just above the water table. As a result, the site often becomes flooded making access difficult, especially in the winter.

Footpath leading from the town along the millstream.

ECONOMIC & FINANCIAL CONSIDERATIONS

As the wood is so small, it has limited economic use. It is too small to receive funding from the Forestry Commission grant schemes. However, as it is a Local Nature Reserve, it may be eligible for funding from Natural England. There is also the possibility of raising small amounts of money by selling pea and bean sticks to people in the nearby allotments.

LEGAL & ENVIRONMENTAL CONSIDERATIONS

The woodland is a Local Nature Reserve, which means it has been recognised by Natural England as an important site for both wildlife and people. It is not a Site of Special Scientific Interest, which means it is not protected by the Wildlife & Countryside Act 1981, nor the Countryside and Rights of Way Act 2000. It also does not have any breeding populations of any European Protected Species (EPS) under the EU Species Directive 1992, although some bats (which are EPS) have been seen within the reserve. It is important that these are encouraged and not disturbed.

None of the trees in the wood are protected by a Tree Preservation Order, so none of the trees are protected by the local authority. Although it would be possible to carry out coppicing and the felling of small trees without permission, no more than 5 cubic metres of larger trees (8 cm diameter at 1.3 m) can be felled in any three month period without a felling licence from the Forestry Commission.

Sample learner work: page 8

Bibliography

Forestry Commission – *Tree Felling: Getting Permission* (Forestry Commission, 2007)
Forestry Commission – *European Protected Species and Woodland operations V3* (Forestry Commission, 2009)
Jones, B, Palmer, J and Sydenham, A – *Countryside Law* (Shaw and Sons, 2004)

Task 3 handout: An evaluation of the 'Colonel Copse Woodland Management Plan' (D2)

Colonel Copse Woodland Management Plan

Site details
Colonel Copse is located along the B3121 outside of the hamlet of Peasley.
Grid Reference: SY 620 135
                                OS 1:50,000 Sheet No. 195
County/District: Peashire
Area: 5.0 acres (2 hectares)
Designations: There are no designations for this site.

Summary site description
Colonel Copse is a recent woodland that was planted on the edge of Peasley in 1952. It was originally owned by the Forestry Commission, who sold it in 1980 to a private landowner hoping to use the land for a woodland holiday park. It was purchased by the Peasley Village Trust in 1999 as a Millennium Project.

The woodland was originally planted with conifers, but these have gradually been removed and the site planted with hardwoods, although some conifers still remain. There are no public footpaths in the wood, but there is a gate from the B3121 onto a permissive footpath and an access track that runs through the wood.

As the wood is located on the edge of the hamlet it is frequently used by local residents. Since the Peasley Village Trust placed a sign at the entrance in 2000 to celebrate the Millennium, there has been a steady increase in visitors from the nearby market town of Woolsager. As there is no car park at the wood, visitors tend to park along the road or by the old chapel, which has been converted into a village hall and is also managed by the Peasley Village Trust.

There are two main compartments in the wood bisected by an access track. When the wood was planted a small pond was created in the lower corner of the wood where the water table is very high. There are no hedgerows linking the wood to any other woodlands. The surrounding land is a mixture of improved grassland for silage/grazing and some houses.

Summary
Colonel Copse is a small wood which is well used by the local people of Peasley. With proper management, it has the potential to be a valuable resource for the community, providing small roundwood produce and open air recreation for several years.

Compartment descriptions

Compartment no.	Area (ha)	Description	Silvicultural Recommendations	Management Constraints	Features	Designations
1	0.40	This is a small corner on the eastern side of the foot path that still retains the original conifer cover. The main species is Douglas fir with a scattering of Scots pine. Some ash has also appeared in the gaps created by a couple of the firs becoming wind-thrown, and these are now approximately 25 cm in diameter, but do not have a good form. The understorey is limited to the woodland and track edges. This consists mainly of elder, hawthorn and blackthorn.	The current management regime is high forest, but it is proposed to clearfell this block of conifers to realise some income for the Peashire Village Trust who are currently fundraising for a new roof on the village hall. Part of the proceeds will also be used to pay for replanting a hazel coppice on this site, as the local residents would like to harvest pea and bean sticks.	Public safety and attitudes. Before any work is planned, the local residents will need to be consulted to get agreement on the felling of the large conifers. Furthermore, access will need to be restricted during the days that the felling operation is taking place.	None	None
2	1.60	This compartment is located on the eastern side of the access track and was planted with broadleaves in 1977 to celebrate the Silver Jubilee. There is a good stocking of oak and ash with the occasional cherry and field maple. Unfortunately, all of the trees are of poor form, particularly the oak, which has been severely damaged by grey squirrels. No management has occurred since the original planting, so the stocking is too dense and there is no understorey or ground flora. In the lower corner of this compartment there is a small pond which is heavily shaded by willow and alder. In the upper corner of the wood, there is a badger sett, which is monitored by the local badger group.	The management regime is high forest with continuous cover. To maintain a suitable stocking level and to improve the diversity of the ground flora, a heavy thinning is recommended, removing the most heavily damaged trees and retaining those least favoured by the squirrels. However, a few wolf trees should be retained to eventually develop into mature veteran trees. The thinnings can be sold to the local villagers or to a firewood contractor. It is recommended that the willow around the pond is pollarded and the alder is coppiced, to allow more light to reach the pond and to reduce the rate of siltation.	The population of grey squirrels will reduce the value of any timber trees. However, they cannot be controlled as the local residents like having them in the wood and many of the residents sit on the Executive Committee of the Peashire Village Trust. The badger sett is also a constraint. It is recommended that the local badger group is consulted prior to any thinning work commencing so that a method of working can be agreed.	Pond Badger sett	None

Note the use of headings to clearly identify the main themes of the text.

As this is a written report, it should start with an introduction about the purpose and scope of the report.

The D2 grading criterion requires that you make. If this was just a critique, it would not achieve the grading criterion.

Sample learner work: page 9

Task 3 learner work: An evaluation of the Colonel Copse Woodland Management Plan (D2)

Title, Site details and Summary site description
No author has been given, so nobody knows who wrote it or where they were from. No date has been given, so nobody knows when the plan was written. Also, it should contain a time span that the plan covers. According to the Forestry Commission, woodland plans should be for a minimum of 5 years.

There are no aims or objectives provided, so nobody knows what the purpose of the woodland is or what the owners want from it. This means that the management recommendations may not be the right ones as they are not connected to any desired outcomes.

The site details are very limited. It would have been useful to have had information on soils, topography or slope, aspect, exposure and geology. Without these details it is difficult to know what are the best trees for the site.

Compartment descriptions
Most of the information is really general. There are recommendations to fell trees, but there are no volume or value estimates. Nor are there any details on replanting or information on potential costs of replanting. This makes it very difficult for the owners to make decisions. No information has been provided on possible sources of funding for small community woodlands.

There are no maps or plans provided that show where the different compartments are or to illustrate the different features. This is particularly important for the badger sett, as it is illegal to disturb a badger sett.

The plan also fails to mention the need for a felling licence. It would be illegal to fell the conifer block without one and the landowners could get in a lot of trouble.

Summary
A summary is provided, but as no objectives have been provided, it is unclear if the recommendations will have the desired outcomes.

No Action Plan has been provided giving recommended activities for the first year. This would have been useful for the owners to have had.

Another useful feature would have been a list of useful contacts. This could have included the names of local timber merchants and forestry contractors, sources of planting stock, sources of grants, the local authority woodland officer, the local Forestry Commission officer and other useful contacts.

Evaluation conclusion
Although this is a good management plan, it is missing several details that would have made it more useful. Some of the missing information could put the owners at risk of breaking the law.

Bibliography
Alexander, M – *Management Planning for Nature Conservation* (Springer, 2007) ISBN 978-1402065804
BTCV and Agate, E – *Woodlands: a practical handbook* (BTCV Enterprises, 2002) ISBN 0946752338
Forestry Commission – Management Plans for Semi-Natural Woodlands Under WGS (Forestry Commission, 2009)
Lane, A and Tait, J – *Practical Conservation: Woodlands* (Open University, 1990) ISBN C1021
Starr, C – *Woodland Management – A Practical Guide* (Crowood Press, 2005) ISBN 978-1861267894
Sutherland, DJ and Hill, WA – *Managing Habitats for Conservation* (Cambridge University Press, 1995) ISBN 978-0521447768

A comprehensive list of sources has been used. Distinction-level work requires evidence of independent study and research.

A clear concise conclusion has been provided to complete the report.

Assessor's comments

This is your opportunity to reflect on your work and any lessons or self-improvement you may have gained as a result of completing the assignment.

Y means that you have provided sufficient evidence to achieve the grading criterion; N means that more work is required as detailed by your tutor.

Qualification	BTEC Level 3 Diploma in Countryside Management	Year	2010–11
Unit number and title	Unit 31: Understanding Woodland Management	Learner name	Jane Doe
Assignment title	Management Planning		

Grading criteria	Achieved?
P8 Explain the structure, content and presentation of a woodland management plan	Y
P9 Explain how to achieve the best balance between present and potential woodland uses covering: i) legal ii) environmental iii) requirements of woodland users iv) economic/financial v) physical	Y
P10 Explain techniques used to assess woodlands	Y
M4 Assess the suitability of a woodland for given activities	Y
D2 Evaluate a selected management plan and suggest improvements	Y

Learner feedback

I don't like talking in front of a group, so I was really dreading the presentation bit of this assignment. However, I felt better once we had done some practising of doing presentations as part of my functional skills classes. The tutors had been talking together, so that I was able to work on this presentation during my functional skills lessons. Once I did the talk I felt a lot better.

Assessor feedback

Jane, thank you for a brilliant assignment. Clearly you have worked very hard on it. Your presentation was clear and well presented – those functional skills lessons have really paid off! Your leaflet is also to a high standard and you have carried out a good evaluation of a management plan.

Action plan

There are just a small number of areas that I would like you to focus on:

1. TASK 3: You have correctly observed that the management plan lacks objectives, but you also omitted to include an introductory paragraph to your own report. Remember that reports should include in introduction that explains the purpose and content of the report.
2. ALL TASKS: Although you have listed your sources, you should get into the habit of actually citing references in the text.

| Assessor signature | *Tamsin Lockthwaite* | Date | *1 July 2011* |
| Learner signature | *Jane Doe* | Date | *8 July 2011* |

You should strive for continuous improvement. Your tutors will provide useful advice to help you achieve the high standards required for your career.

Step Seven: Work productively as a member of a group

Case study: Team working

Jane is very excited. She has been invited for an interview at a safari park for a position that involves looking after the big cats – lions and tigers. Jane is quite nervous as although she learned about lions and tigers as part of her BTEC Level 3 National in Animal Management, she has little experience of caring for them.

However, when Jane gets to the interview, the panel isn't really interested that she doesn't have much experience. The manager explains that it is most unusual for applicants to have all the handling skills required, which is why all new employees undergo a thorough training programme. She goes on to say that the key to successful employment at the park, particularly when working with animals, is teamwork. Each member of the cat team needs to know they can rely on the other members to carry out their roles responsibly and to provide effective communication and support – otherwise lives could be at risk.

The key question for the interview panel, the one that helps to separate the stronger candidate from the weaker ones, is 'Please tell us about one or two recent experiences of your role and participation within a team'.

Jane tells them about several experiences where she has worked within a small team as part of her BTEC Level 3 National in Animal Management, including teamwork when moving groups of animals. However, the one she focuses on is when she and two other students did a poster presentation comparing the behaviour of wild and domestic cats. Jane has brought a copy of the poster with her, so she is able to talk about the project and her role in it. She also mentions what she has learned from the experience, not just about cats, but also about the importance (and some of the potential problems) of working in teams.

Reflection points

Do you think Jane got the job? If so, why was she successful?

In your private life, you can choose your own friends, whereas at work you are paid to work alongside many people, whether you like them or not. This applies at school or college too. Hopefully, by now, you've outgrown wanting to only work with your best friends on every project.

You may not be keen on everyone in your team, but you should still be pleasant and co-operative. This may be harder if you are working with a partner than in a large group.

Sometimes you may be the group leader. This may inspire you, or fill you with dread. You won't be expected to develop team-leader skills overnight, but it helps if you know the basics.

First, you should understand how groups and teams work and why good teamwork is considered vital by employers.

Working in groups and teams

If you have a full-time or part-time job, you already belong to a working group, or team. At school or college your class is an example of a working group.

All working groups have some common characteristics:

- doing the same type of work – though in the workplace you probably have different roles or responsibilities
- a group leader or supervisor
- a reason for working together, such as studying for the same qualification or tackling an area of work too large for someone to do alone
- group members are dependent on each other in some way; at work you may have to cover someone's workload if they are absent
- group members concentrate on their individual achievements and success.

A team is different. As a team member you have a specific objective to achieve **together** – and this is more important than the goals of individual team members.

These are the characteristics of a team.

- Team members have a team goal which is more important than any personal goals.
- Team members have complementary skills so that the team can achieve more than individuals working alone could achieve.
- Work is allocated to play to each person's strengths and talents.
- The team members give each other encouragement and support.
- There is collective responsibility for achieving the goal.

A good team leader acts as facilitator and motivator, and gives practical support and guidance.

Working in a team has many benefits. Team members can learn from each other and combine their skills to do a better job more quickly. Working with other people is often more enjoyable than working alone, too. Many industries rely heavily on efficient group working, from IT teams to health workers and the emergency services.

TOP TIP

Understanding how groups and teams function will help you be a better team worker and a better team leader.

TOP TIP

Focusing on the task rather than on personalities is the first step in learning to work with different people, whose views may not match your own.

There are many benefits to be gained from working as a team.

Being a good team member

Everyone wants team members who are talented, positive, cheerful and full of energy. These are the key areas to focus on if you wish to be a good team member.

- **Your social skills.** This includes being courteous, treating other people as you wish to be treated, saying 'please' when you want something and thanking people who do you a favour.

- **Your temperament**. Expect people to have different views and opinions from you and don't take offence if someone disagrees with you. If you lose your temper easily, learn to walk away before you say something you may regret.

- **Your communication skills.** This includes talking and listening!

Practise saying what you mean clearly, accurately and succinctly. Be prepared to give good reasons to justify your arguments and ideas.

Allow people to finish what they're saying, without interruption, before you talk. Never shout people down. Think before you speak so that you don't upset people with tactless remarks. If you inadvertently do so, apologise.

- **Your commitment.** Always keep your promises and never let anyone down when they are depending upon you. Always do your fair share of the work, even if you don't agree with all the decisions made by your team. Tell people promptly if you are having problems so there is time to solve them. Be loyal to your team when you're talking to other people.

Being the team leader

It can be difficult to strike a balance between 'leading' the team and working with friends. You need to inspire and motivate your team without being bossy or critical.

Important points to remember about being a team leader

- Lead by example. Stay pleasant, consistent and control your temper, even under pressure.
- Everyone is different. Your ways of working may not always be the best.
- Be prepared to listen and contribute positively to a discussion.
- Encourage quieter team members to join in discussions by asking for their views.
- Be prepared to do whatever you ask other people to do.
- Note down what you say you will do, so that you don't forget.
- Discuss alternatives with people rather than giving orders.
- Be sensitive to other people's feelings. They may have personal problems or issues that affect their behaviour.
- Learn the art of persuasion.
- Act as peacemaker. Help people reach a compromise when necessary.
- Give team members the credit for their hard work or good ideas.
- Admit your mistakes. Look for a positive solution and think about what can be learned for the future, rather than making excuses.
- Praise and encourage team members who are working hard.
- Make criticisms constructively, and in private.
- Be assertive (put forward your point of view firmly) rather than aggressive (attacking other people to defend yourself).

Some notes of caution about being a team leader

- Try to look pleasant and don't glare at people who interrupt you unexpectedly.
- Never talk about team members behind their backs.
- Don't gossip, exaggerate to make a point, spread rumours, speculate or tell lies.
- Don't expect to get your own way all the time – all good leaders back down on occasion.
- Never criticise any colleagues in front of other people. Speak to them in private and keep it constructive.

TOP TIP

Excellent ideas often come from quiet team members. Encourage everyone to make suggestions so that you don't overlook any valuable contributions.

Key points

- There are many benefits of working in a group or as a team. These include mutual support, companionship and the exchange of ideas.
- You will be expected to work co-operatively with other people at work, and during many course assignments.
- It isn't easy learning to be a team leader. Team leaders should be fair, consistent and pleasant to work with, as well as loyal and sensitive to the needs of team members.

Action points

1 Identify the role of teamwork in your area of study. Identify the team's goal and any factors you think will contribute towards its success.

2 Decide how you would handle each of the following difficult situations if you were the team leader. If you can, discuss your ideas with a friend in your class.

   a) The team needs to borrow a college video camera to record an event being held tonight. Your tutor tells you that the one you reserved last week is not working and the rest are out on loan.

   b) A member of your team has personal problems so you have given him less work to do. Now you've been accused of having favourites.

   c) A team member is constantly letting everyone down because of poor work and non-attendance at group meetings.

   d) Two team members have disagreed about how to do a task. You're not bothered how they do it as long as it gets done properly, and by the deadline.

   e) A team member becomes very aggressive whenever she is challenged in any way – no matter how mildly.

3 Identify someone who has inspired you because they've been an excellent leader. This could be someone you've met, a fictional character or a famous person. Note down what it is about them that impressed you.

TOP TIP

Team working, and bouncing ideas around, produces quicker and better results than working in isolation. Land and Environment businesses actively encourage team working.

Activity: Team working

Sam is part of a group of four learners carrying out a river study. The group has equipment to measure the physical characteristics of the river, as well as several books to identify some of the wildlife that they find. Sam has never done anything like this, so is happy for the others to take the lead. That's okay, but what should Sam be doing?

1.	
2.	

What is likely to happen if Sam isn't more involved?

1.	
2.	
3.	

What do you think Sam is missing out on if he doesn't actively involve himself?

1.	
2.	
3.	

TOP TIPS

Remember – you are part of a team as well as an individual, so you will need to establish a balance between the two.

Step Eight: Understand how to research and analyse information

Case study: Learning both sides of an argument

Zoe is an animal lover. She belongs to several wildlife groups. As part of a wildlife conservation unit on her BTEC Level 3 National in Animal Management, Zoe is asked to write an assignment on the importance of killing animals, such as deer, to control their numbers.

Zoe can't possibly see how killing animals can ever be justified. She is a strict vegetarian and believes that all animals have a right to live. In her research, she finds plenty of support from the documents produced by the organisations that she belongs to.

The only problem is that the assignment requires learners to provide a balanced and justified argument. Zoe goes to the library and finds a countryside sports magazine. This tends to focus more on the 'how' rather than the 'why', so it is not much use, although she has picked up a few points from her quick skim. She finds a textbook in the library that points out that most of the deer in Britain originally came from other countries. As a result, they compete with native species and cause habitat disruption.

Still not convinced that deer deserve to be killed just because some of them are not native, Zoe looks at scientific journals on nature conservation and conservation biology. She reads studies where deer numbers have mushroomed out of control and the deer have destroyed valuable wildlife habitats. She also reads about large numbers dying from disease, starvation and road accidents as a result of overpopulation.

Having gathered her evidence, Zoe feels ready to complete her assignment. Although she can see both sides of the argument, she still doesn't like to see animals being killed. She also doesn't like to see them suffering through disease and starvation, so she accepts that some control measures may be required. However, she advocates killing only as a last resort and recommends alternative measures, such as sterilisation, which she has read is used in other countries.

Reflection points

What are your thoughts about this? If you need more information to make your decision, where would you find it?

As a BTEC Level 3 National learner, you often have to find information for yourself. This skill will be invaluable in your working life, and if you continue your studies at higher education level. Sometimes the information will give you a better understanding of a topic, at other times you will research information for a project or assignment. Sometimes you may be so interested in something that you want to find out more without being told to do so!

Whatever your reason, and no matter where your information can be found, there is a good and not so good way to go about the task. This section

TOP TIPS

When reading newspapers and magazines or browsing the internet, look out for newsworthy stories about what's happening around the world that might impact on your studies.

will help if you can't find what you want, or find too much, or drift aimlessly around a library, or watch a demonstration and don't know what to ask afterwards.

Types of information

There are many types of information and many different sources. Depending on the task, these are the sources you may need to consult.

- **Verbal information.** This includes talking to friends, colleagues at work, members of your family, listening to experts explain what they do, interviewing people, talking to sales reps at an exhibition or customers about a product.

- **Printed information.** This includes information printed in newspapers, journals, magazines, books, posters, workshop manuals, leaflets and catalogues. The type of magazine or newspaper you read may have its own slant on the information, which you may have to take into account (see page 73).

- **Written information.** This includes course notes and handouts, reports and other documents in the workplace. If you want to use written information from work, you must check this is allowed, and that it doesn't contain confidential material such as financial information or staff names and addresses.

- **Graphical information.** This includes illustrations, pictures, cartoons, line drawings, graphs and photographs. Graphics can make something clearer than words alone. For example, a satnav instruction book might contain illustrations to show different procedures.

- **Electronic information.** This includes information from electronic sources such as DVDs, CD-ROMs, searchable databases, websites, podcasts, webinars (**seminars** online), emails and text messages. The huge amount of information available online is both a help and a hindrance. You can find information quickly, but the source may be unreliable, out of date, inaccurate or inappropriate (see page 66.)

TOP TIP

Too much information is as bad as too little, because it's overwhelming. The trick is to find good quality, relevant information and know when to call a halt to your search.

TOP TIP

Consider all appropriate sources and don't just rely on information found online.

Finding what you need

Spend a few minutes planning what to do before you start looking for information. This can save a lot of time later on.

The following steps will help you to do this.

1 Make sure you understand exactly what it is you need to know so that you don't waste time looking for the wrong thing.

2 Clarify your objectives to narrow down your search. Think about why the information is wanted and how much detail you need. For example, learners studying BTEC Nationals in Engineering and Performing Arts may both be researching 'noise' for their projects but they are likely to need different types of information and use it in different ways.

3 Identify your sources and check you know how to use them. You need to choose sources that are most likely to provide information relevant to your objectives. For example, an engineering learner might find information on noise emissions in industry journals and by checking out specialist websites.

4 Plan and schedule your research. Theoretically, you could research information forever. Knowing when to call a halt takes skill. Write a schedule that states when you must stop looking and start sorting the information.

5 Store your information safely in a labelled folder. This folder should include printouts or photocopies of articles, notes about events you have attended or observed, photographs you've taken or sketches you've drawn. Divide your information under topic headings to make it easier to find. When you're ready to start work, re-read your assignment brief and select the items that are most closely related to the task you are doing.

TOP TIP

Allocate time for research as part of your assignment task. Take into account any interim deadlines as well as the final deadline for completing the work.

Primary and secondary research, and the law of copyright

There are two ways to research information. One is known as primary research, the other is secondary research.

Primary research

Primary research involves finding new information about an issue or topic. This might include finding out people's views about a product or interviewing an expert. When carrying out interviews, you will need to design a survey or questionnaire. Your primary research might also include observing or experiencing something for yourself, and recording your feelings and observations.

Secondary research

Secondary research involves accessing information that already exists in books, files, newspapers or on CD-ROMs, computer databases or the internet, and assessing it against your objectives.

This information has been prepared by other people and is available to anyone. You can quote from an original work provided you acknowledge the source of your information. You should put this acknowledgement in your text or in the bibliography to your text; do not claim it as your own research. You must include the author's name, year of publication, the title and publisher, or the web address if it is an online article. You should practise listing the sources of articles so

that you feel confident writing a bibliography. Use the guidance sheet issued by your centre to help you. This will illustrate the style your centre recommends.

The trick with research is to choose the best technique to achieve your objectives and this may mean using a mix of methods and resources. For example, if you have to comment on an industry event you might go to it, make notes, interview people attending, observe the event (perhaps take a video camera), and read any newspaper reports or online comments.

TOP TIP

Always make sure you make a note of where you get information from (your source). Keep it safely as it can be very difficult later on to work out where it came from!

People as a source of information

If you want to get the most out of interviewing someone, or several people, you need to prepare carefully in advance.

The following points give some general advice about getting the most out of face-to-face interviews.

- Make sure you know what questions to ask to get the information you need.
- Explain why you want the information.
- Don't expect to be told confidential or sensitive information.
- Write clear notes so that you remember who told you what, and when. (See also page 68.)
- Note the contact details of the person you are interviewing and ask whether they mind if you contact them again should you think of anything later or need to clarify your notes.
- Thank them for their help.

If you want to ask a lot of people for their opinion, you may want to conduct a survey. You will need to design a questionnaire and analyse the results. This will be easier if you ask for **quantitative** responses – for example yes/no, true/false or ratings on a five-point scale – rather than opinions.

- Give careful thought to your representative sample (people whose opinions are relevant to the topic).

- Decide how many people to survey so that the results mean something.

- Keep the survey relatively short.

- Thank people who complete it.

- Analyse the results, and write up your conclusions promptly.

TOP TIP

Test your questionnaire on volunteers before you 'go live' to check that there are no mistakes and the questions are easy to understand. Make any amendments before you conduct your 'real' survey.

Asking someone who knows a lot about a topic can be informative.

Avoiding pitfalls

Wikipedia is a good online source that covers many topics, and often in some depth. It is popular and free. However, it has an open-content policy, which means that anyone can contribute to and edit entries. People may post information, whether it is correct or not. Wikipedia is moving towards greater checks on entries, but it is still sensible to check out information you find on this site somewhere else.

Apart from inaccuracy, there are other problems that you may find with any information you obtain through research, especially material found online.

- **Out-of-date material.** Check the date of everything and keep only the latest version of books, newspapers or magazines. Yesterday's news may be of little use if you are researching something topical.

- **Irrelevant details.** Often, only part of an article will be relevant to your search. For example, if you are forecasting future trends in an area of work, you do not need information about its history or related problems. When learners are struggling, they sometimes 'pad out' answers with irrelevant information. If you've researched properly you can avoid this by having enough relevant information for your purposes.

- **Invalid assumptions.** This means someone has jumped to the wrong conclusion and made 2 + 2 = 5. You might do this if you see two friends chatting and think they are talking about you – whether they are or not! You can avoid problems in this area by double-checking your ideas and getting evidence to support them.

- **Bias.** This is when people hold strong views about a topic, or let their emotions or prejudices affect their judgement. An obvious example is asking a keen football fan for an objective evaluation of their team's performance!

- **Vested interests.** People may argue in a certain way because it's in their own interests to do so. For example, when the government said Home Information Packs must be prepared for all properties being sold, the Association of Home Information Pack Providers was in favour because it trains the people who prepare the packs. The National Association of Estate Agents and Royal Institution of Chartered Surveyors were not because they thought they would lose business if people were put off selling their houses.

> **TOP TIP**
>
> Don't discard information that is affected by bias or vested interests. Just make it clear you know about the problem and have taken it into account.

Reading for a purpose

You may enjoy reading or you may find it tedious or difficult. If so, it helps to know that there are different ways to read, depending on what you're doing. For example, you wouldn't look for a programme in a TV guide in the same way that you would check an assignment for mistakes. You can save time and find information more easily if you use the best method of reading to suit your purpose. The following are some examples of ways of reading.

- **Skim reading** is used to check new information and get a general overview.
  To skim a book chapter read the first and last paragraphs, the headings, subheadings and illustrations. It also helps to read the first sentence of each paragraph.

> **TOP TIP**
>
> News articles are written with the key points at the beginning, so concentrate on the first paragraph or two. Feature articles have a general introduction and important information is contained in the main text.

- **Scanning** is used to see whether an article contains something you need – such as key words, dates or technical terms.
  Focus on capital or initial letters for a name, and figures for a date. Technical terms may be in bold or italics.

- **Light reading** is usually done for pleasure when you are relaxed, for example, reading a magazine article. You may not remember many facts afterwards, so this sort of reading isn't suitable for learning something or assessing its value.

- **Word-by-word reading (proofreading)** is important so that you don't miss anything, such as the dosage instructions for a strong medicine. You should proofread assignments before you submit them.

- **Reading for study (active reading)** means being actively involved so that you understand the information. It is rare to be naturally good at this, so you might have to work to develop this skill.

Developing critical and analytical skills

Developing critical and analytical skills involves looking at information for any flaws in the arguments. These skills are important when you progress to work or higher education (HE), so it's useful to practise them now on your BTEC Level 3 National course.

A useful technique for understanding, analysing, evaluating and remembering what you are reading is **SQ4R**.

SQ4R is an effective method. It consists of six steps.

1 Survey first, to get a general impression. Scan the information to see what it is about, when it was written and by whom. The source, and the reason it was written, may be important. Most newspapers, for example, have their own 'slant' that affects how information is presented.

2 Question your aims for reading this material. What are you hoping to find? What questions are you expecting it to answer?

3 Read the information three or four times. The first time, aim to get a general idea of the content. Use a dictionary to look up any new words. Then read more carefully to really understand what the writer means.

4 Respond by thinking critically about the information and how it relates to the topic you are studying. Does it answer your queries partially, fully or not at all? What information is factual and what is based on opinion? Is there evidence to support these opinions? Is there a reason why the author has taken this standpoint? Do you agree with it? How does it link to other information you have read? What is the opposite argument and is there any evidence to support this? Overall, how useful is this information?

5 Record the information by noting the key points. Use this to refresh your memory, if necessary, rather than re-reading the article.

6 Review your notes against the original to check you have included all important points. If you are also preparing a presentation, reviewing your notes will help you to remember key points more easily.

TOP TIP

SQ4R is just one method of reading for study. Research others and adapt them to suit your own style.

Taking good notes

There are many occasions when you need to take notes, such as when a visiting speaker is talking to your class. There's no point taking notes unless you write them in a way that will allow you to use them later.

Note-taking is a personal activity. Some people prefer to make diagrammatical sketches with key points in boxes linked by arrows, others prefer to write a series of bullet points. You will develop your own style, but the following hints and tips might help you at the start.

- Use A4 lined paper, rather than a notebook, so that you have more space and don't need to turn over so often.
- When you're reading for study, make sure you have a dictionary, pen, notepad and highlighter to hand.
- Leave a wide margin to record your own comments or queries.
- Put a heading at the top, such as the speaker's name and topic, as well as the date.
- If you are making notes from a book or an article, remember SQ4R and read it several times first. Your notes will only be effective if you understand the information.
- Don't write in complete sentences – it takes too long.
- Leave spaces for later additions or corrections.
- Use headings to keep your notes clear and well organised.
- Only write down relevant information, including key words and phrases.

- Highlight, underline or use capitals for essential points.
- Never copy chunks of text – always use your own words.
- Clearly identify quotations, and record your sources, so that you can cite them in your work. (Note the author's name, title, publisher, date and place of publication and the page number.)

TOP TIP

Make sure your information is accurate, up to date, relevant and valid. Be aware of bias, and don't confuse fact with opinion.

Key points

- Useful information may be verbal, printed, written, graphical or electronic.
- Effective research means knowing exactly what you are trying to find and where to look. Know how reference media are stored in your library and how to search online. Store important information carefully.
- Primary research is original data you obtain yourself. Secondary research is information prepared by someone else. If you use this, you must quote your sources in a bibliography.
- You can search for information by skimming and scanning, and read in different ways. Reading for study means actively involving yourself with the text, questioning what you are reading and making notes to help your own understanding.
- Read widely around a topic to get different viewpoints. Don't accept everything you read as correct. Think about how it fits with other information you have obtained.
- Taking notes is a personal skill that takes time to develop. Start by using A4 lined pages with a margin, set out your notes clearly and label them. Only record essential information.

Action points

- Working with a friend, look back at the sources of information listed on page 64. For each type, identify examples of information relevant to your course that you could obtain from each source. See how many you can list under each type.
- Check your ability to find the information you need by answering each of the questions in **Activity: Finding information** on the next page. For any questions you get wrong, your first research task is to find out the correct answers as quickly as you can.
- Go to page 94 to find out how you can access a website where you can check your ability to skim and scan information, improve your ability to differentiate fact from opinion, summarise text, and much more.
- Check your ability to sort fact from opinion and spot vested interests by completing **Activity: Let's give you a tip...** on page 72. Check your ideas with the answers on page 95.

TOP TIP

Make a note of any information that you are struggling to understand so that you can discuss it with your tutor.

Activity: Finding information

Answer the following questions about finding information.

a) Four types of information that are available from the library in your centre, besides books, are:

1

2

3

4

b) When I visit the library, the way to check if a book I want is available is:

c) The difference between borrowing a book on short-term loan and on long-term loan is:

Short-term loan:

Long-term loan:

d) The journals that are stocked by the library that are relevant to my course include:

e) Useful information on the intranet at my centre includes:

f) Searchable databases and online magazines I can access include:

g) The quickest way to check if a book or journal contains the type of information I need is to:

h) The difference between a search engine, a portal, a directory site and a forum is:

i) Bookmarking useful websites means:

j) In addition to suggesting websites, Google can also provide the following types of information:

k) Specialist websites which provide useful information related to my course include:

l) Useful tips I would give to people starting on my course who need to find out information are:

Activity: Let's give you a tip...

In 2009, many businesses were struggling thanks to the credit crunch and falling consumer demand. Some, like Woolworths, closed down altogether. Others laid off staff, or announced wage cuts. Despite this, the government approved recommendations by the Low Pay Commission to increase the minimum wage rate from October. Although the rise was only small, many unions, including Unison and Usdaw, agreed it was better than a freeze, which had been wanted by the British Chambers of Commerce and the British Retail Consortium.

The government also announced new laws to stop restaurants and bars using tips to top up staff pay to the minimum level. *The Independent* newspaper claimed its 'fair tips, fair pay' campaign had won the day. It also reported that the British Hospitality Association was claiming this could result in up to 45,000 job losses. The Unite union also carried out a campaign and its General Secretary claimed the decision a triumph for the poorly paid. Not everyone agreed. Some thought there should be no tipping at all, as in Australia. Others said the Canadian system was best – wages are low but generous tips are left, and this motivates staff to give excellent service.

a) Look at the table below. In your view, which of the statements are facts and which are opinions? In each case, justify your view.

Statement	Fact or opinion?	Justification
i) Having a national minimum wage helps low-paid workers.		
ii) Over one million people will benefit from the minimum wage increase.		
iii) The new law on tips will stop restaurants paying below minimum wage rates.		
iv) Using the Australian system of no tips would be better.		
v) The Canadian system guarantees good service.		
vi) 45,000 job losses will occur in the hospitality industry.		

b) All newspapers have their own way of putting forward the news. Go to page 96 to find out how to access a website for this page. From here, you can access a website which will help you to compare the way that news is reported in different newspapers.

Compare six different newspapers and make notes on:

i) the type of stories covered

ii) the way views are put forward.

Activity: Resources

As part of a BTEC National in Agriculture, Carl is working on an assignment that covers the different breeds of sheep that are raised in the UK. Fortunately, the centre library has a wide range of sources available for Carl to use. Below are the main types of resources that can be found in the library. Can you identify the main advantages and disadvantages for each type?

Source	Advantages	Disadvantages
Internet		
Textbook		
Magazine		
Journal		

Step Nine: Make an effective presentation

Case study: Preparing for your presentation

Every year at the centre where Jordan is doing her BTEC Level 3 National in Horticulture, an Apple Day is held. It is really popular and people come from a wide area to have their apples identified, taste some local cider, purchase apples and trees, and learn more about how to grow them. All the students help organise and run the event, which forms an important part of their course assessment. This year, the tutor asks Jordan to lead the demonstration of apple-tree pruning.

Jordan is quite happy with the pruning aspect, but less happy speaking in front of the general public. She likes horticulture because plants don't talk back!

However, Jordan is pleased that her tutor has asked her to do the demonstration, so she sets about getting ready. She takes the tools out of the tool store, checking first that they are sharp and ready to use.

Her next step is to look at the trees to be sure she is confident about the job. She knows them well as she has had lots of practice on them.

The technical side is covered; but Jordan needs to make sure that everyone can see and hear her? She asks her tutor for some pointers. He shows her where she should stand and where she should direct the audience to stand. He then stands in the imaginary crowd and tells her to introduce herself and describe what she is doing. On several occasions, he directs her to speak louder, but eventually, Jordan settles into speaking loud and clear.

Jordan spends an hour practising her demonstration in front of the mirror until she finds a speaking style that she is happy with.

When giving a demonstration, it is difficult to refer to notes. In order to ensure that the audience picks up all the important points, Jordan prepares a handout for them to take home. It also provides useful evidence for her forthcoming assignment.

Reflection points

Do you think Jordan is ready?

Making a presentation can be nerve-wracking. It involves several skills, including planning, preparation and communication. It tests your ability to work in a team, speak in public and use IT (normally PowerPoint). You also have to stay calm under pressure. However, as it is excellent practice for your future, you can expect presentations to be a common method of assessing your performance.

TOP TIP

When giving a presentation, keep to time, get to the point and use your time well.

Good planning and preparation

Being well prepared, and rehearsing beforehand, helps your confidence and your presentation. The following points will help you to do this.

- If you're part of a team, find out everyone's strengths and weaknesses and divide work fairly taking these into account. Decide how long each person should speak, who should introduce the team and who will summarise at the end.

- Take into account the time you have been allocated, your resources and team skills. A simple, clear presentation is better – and safer – than a complicated one.

- If you're using PowerPoint, make slides more interesting by avoiding a series of bulleted lists and including artwork. Print PowerPoint notes for the audience. Use a fuller set of notes for yourself, as a prompt.

- Check the venue and time.

- Decide what to wear and check it's clean and presentable.

- Prepare, check and print your handouts.

- Decide, as a team, the order in which people will speak, bearing in mind the topic.

- Discuss possible questions and how to answer them.

- Rehearse beforehand to check your timings.

If you prepare properly, you can really enjoy giving a presentation.

TOP TIP

Rehearsing properly allows you to speak fluently, just glancing at your notes to remind you of the next key point.

On the day, you can achieve a better performance if you:

- arrive in plenty of time
- calm your nerves by taking deep breaths before going in front of your audience
- introduce yourself clearly, and smile at the audience
- avoid reading from your screen or your notes
- explain what you are going to do – especially if giving a demonstration – do it and then review what you've done
- say you will deal with questions at the end of any demonstration
- answer questions honestly – don't exaggerate, guess or waffle
- respond positively to all feedback, which should be used to improve your performance next time.

TOP TIPS

Make sure you can be heard clearly by lifting your head and speaking a little more slowly and loudly than normal.

Key points

- When making a presentation, prepare well, don't be too ambitious and have several rehearsals.
- When giving a demonstration, explain first what you are going to do and that you will answer questions at the end.

Case study: Learner quotes about making presentations

Most people start off feeling uncomfortable about talking in front of a group of people, whether you know them or not. This is what some real learners have said about having to give presentations as part of their BTEC course.

"I actually feel more comfortable giving a presentation rather than having to write an essay. What I really enjoy about it is the fact that sometimes we have to prepare a presentation as a whole group. I like that we work together to find information and then we take turns presenting different points. The fact that I am not the only one out there and I am part of a supportive team makes it fun for me."

Gabriela, 16, BTEC Level 2 First in Performing Arts

"Although presentations are very stressful, when I present my work it helps to hang my ideas together and I find I can express what I want to say more clearly than when I write things down. Instant feedback is helpful and boosts my confidence for the next time."

Ethan, 19, BTEC Level 2 First in Creative Media Production

"I think presentations are useful but I find them difficult to deliver - relying heavily on my memory, which is very nerve-racking. We were told that presentation would be part of our assessment. I really worried about it and couldn't sleep the night before – stressing out about what I was going to say. I hated the first few minutes, but after that I was OK."

Will, 16, BTEC Level 2 First in Engineering

"I was very nervous about presenting to my class until I took part in the Young Enterprise scheme and had to present the results of our project to over 200 people including the mayor! After that presenting to my class mates didn't feel too nerve wracking at all."

Lizzy, 17, BTEC Level 2 First in Business

"I used to dread presentations on my course, but found that if I went through my notes again and again until I knew the presentation inside out, it made it much easier and the presentations generally went well."

Javinder, 17, BTEC Level 3 National in Construction

Activity: All right on the night?

Read the following account and answer the questions that follow. If possible, compare ideas with a friend in your class.

Gemma looked around in exasperation. The team were on the final rehearsal of their presentation and nothing was going right. Amaya seemed to think it was funny. 'Honestly, Gemma, why don't you just chill for a bit?' she suggested. 'You know what they say – a bad dress rehearsal means we'll do really well tomorrow!'

Gemma glared at her. 'Well, can I make a suggestion, too, Amaya,' she retorted. 'Why don't you just concentrate for a change? Sprawling around and dissolving into giggles every five minutes isn't helping either.'

She turned to Adam. 'And I thought you were going to build a simple model,' she said, 'not one that falls apart every time you touch it.'

Adam looked crest-fallen. 'But I wanted to show how it worked.'

'How it's supposed to work, you mean!' raged Gemma, all her worries and anxieties now coming to the fore. 'We'll look stupid if it ends up in bits on the floor tomorrow and Amaya just falls about laughing again.'

'And Imran,' continued Gemma, turning her sights on the last member of the team, 'why is it so difficult for you to count to three minutes? We've agreed over and over again we'll each talk for three minutes and every time you get carried away with the sound of your own voice and talk for twice as long. It just means we're going to overrun and get penalised. And stop trying to wriggle out of answering questions properly. For heaven's sake, if you don't know the answer, how hard is it just to say so?'

Silence fell. No-one looked at each other. Adam fiddled with his model and something else fell off. Amaya wanted to laugh but didn't dare.

Imran was sulking and vowed never to say anything ever again. 'You wait,' he thought. 'Tomorrow I'll race through my part in one minute flat. And then what are you going to do?'

1   Identify the strengths and weaknesses of each member of the presentation team.

Name	Strengths	Weaknesses
Gemma		
Amaya		
Adam		
Imran		

2 What have the team done right, so far, in getting ready for their presentation?

3 Why do you think they are having problems?

4 If you were Gemma's tutor, what advice would you give her at this point?

Activity: Making sure you're prepared

As part of her BTEC Level 3 National in Countryside Management, Rose needs to lead a guided walk around a local woodland. Her class has recently visited the woodland, so she knows something about it. However, the more she thinks about it, the more she realises that there is still quite a bit that she doesn't know. For example, the tutor took them all over the wood; there were lots of turns, plus some very steep parts. Rose isn't sure that she can remember the route, nor is she sure that it would be the most suitable, so she decides to visit the woodland again.

In the table below, record three things that Rose should look out for when she is there.

1.	
2.	
3.	

What else do you think Rose should do to prepare?

TOP TIPS

When making a PowerPoint presentation, don't just read out what it says on the slides. The audience can do this. Use the slides as prompt cards.

Step Ten: Maximise your opportunities and manage your problems

Case study: How Calum is dealing with his problems

Calum is taking a BTEC Level 3 National in Horticulture and has an assignment on plant nutrition. However, Calum has twisted his ankle playing football and missed several sessions covering plant nutrition.

His Mum phones the centre and speaks to the tutor. They agree a revised set of submission dates for Calum's assignments. This takes some of the pressure off. The centre and family are working together to ensure Calum's success.

Calum has a good friend at the centre who also lives nearby. He pops in on Calum regularly to see how he is and to pass on notes, handouts and any other useful information.

Calum has a good internet connection at home that allows him to check out websites for information and he can visit the centre's own website to track down some useful books that his friend can collect from the centre's library.

The centre's website has a comprehensive student section that includes information on all the courses. Calum's tutor has a section there which has some good resources that Calum can download for his assignment.

Calum may not be able to go into the centre, but he can still get all the information he needs.

Reflection points

Apart from understanding and sympathetic friends, family and tutors, what do you think is the most essential personal trait required to get you through a crisis?

If your course takes one or two years to complete, then it is highly likely that you will experience some highs and lows in that time. You may find one or two topics harder than the rest. There may be distractions in your personal life to cope with. All of which means than you may not always be able to do your best.

It is, therefore, sensible to have an action plan to help you cope. It's also wise to plan how to make the best of opportunities for additional

experiences or learning. This section shows you how to do this.

TOP TIP

Because life rarely runs smoothly, it's sensible to capitalise on the opportunities that come your way and have a plan to deal with problems.

Making the most of your opportunities

There will be many opportunities for learning on your course, not all of which will be in school or college. You should prepare for some of the following to maximise the opportunities that each offer.

- **External visits**. Prepare in advance by reading about relevant topics. Make notes when you are there. Write up your notes neatly and file them safely for future reference.

- **Visiting speakers**. Questions can usually be submitted to the speaker in advance. Think carefully about information that you would find helpful. Make notes, unless someone has been appointed to make notes for the whole group. You may be asked to thank the speaker on behalf of your group.

- **Work experience**. If work experience is an essential part of your course, your tutor will help you to organise your placement and tell you about the evidence you need to obtain. You may also get a special logbook in which to record your experiences. Read and re-read the units to which your evidence will apply and make sure you understand the grading criteria and what you need to obtain. Make time to write up your notes, logbook and/or diary every night (if possible), while everything is fresh in your mind.

- **In your own workplace**. If you have a full-time or part-time job, watch for opportunities to find out more about relevant topics that relate to your course, such as health and safety, teamwork, dealing with customers, IT security and communications. Your employer will have had to address all of these issues. Finding out more about these issues will broaden your knowledge and give more depth to your assessment responses.

- **Television, newspapers, podcasts and other information sources**. The media can be an invaluable source of information. Look out for news bulletins relating to your studies, as well as information in topical television programmes – from *The Apprentice* to *Top Gear*. You can also read news headlines online. Podcasts are useful, too. It will help if you know what topics you will be studying in the months to come, so you can spot useful opportunities as they arise.

> **TOP TIP**
>
> Remember that you can use online catch-up services, such as the BBC iPlayer or 4oD (for Channel 4 shows) to see TV programmes you have missed recently.

Minimising problems

Hopefully, any problems you experience during your course will only be minor; such as struggling to find an acceptable working method with someone in your team.

You should already know who to talk to about these issues, and who to go to if that person is absent or you would prefer to talk to someone else. If your problems are affecting your work, it's sensible to see your tutor promptly. It is a rare learner who is enthusiastic about every topic and gets on well with everyone else doing the course, so your tutor won't be surprised and will give you useful guidance (in confidence) to help.

> **TOP TIP**
>
> Don't delay talking to someone in confidence if you have a serious problem. If your course tutor is unavailable, talk to another staff member you like and trust.

Other sources of help

If you are unfortunate enough to have a more serious personal problem, the following sources of help may be available in your centre.

- **Professional counselling.** There may be a professional counselling service. If you see a counsellor, nothing you say during the session can be mentioned to another member of staff without your permission.

- **Complaint procedures.** If you have a serious complaint, the first step is to talk to your tutor. If you can't resolve your problem informally, there will be a formal learner complaint procedure. These procedures are used only for serious issues, not for minor difficulties.

- **Appeals procedures.** If you disagree with your final grade for an assignment, check the grading criteria and ask the subject tutor to explain how the grade was awarded. If you are still unhappy, talk to your personal tutor. If you still disagree, you have the right to make a formal appeal.

- **Disciplinary procedures.** These exist for when learners consistently flout a centre's rules and ensure that all learners are dealt with in the same way. Hopefully, you will never get into trouble, but you should make sure that you read these procedures carefully to see what could happen if you did. Remember that being honest and making a swift apology is always the wisest course of action.

- **Serious illness.** Whether this involves you, a family member or a close friend, it could affect your attendance. Discuss the problem with your tutor promptly; you will be missing information from the first day you are absent. There are many solutions in this type of situation – such as sending notes by post and updating you electronically (providing you are well enough to cope with the work).

TOP TIP

It's important to know your centre's procedures for dealing with important issues such as complaints, major illnesses, learner appeals and disciplinary matters.

Key points

- Don't miss opportunities to learn more about relevant topics through external visits, listening to visiting speakers, work experience, being at work or even watching television.

- If you have difficulties or concerns, talk to your tutor, or another appropriate person, promptly to make sure your work isn't affected.

Action points

1 Prepare in advance to maximise your opportunities.
  a) List the opportunities available on your course for obtaining more information and talking to experts. You can check with your tutor to make sure you've identified them all.

  b) Check the content of each unit you will be studying so that you know the main topics and focus of each.

  c) Identify the information that may be relevant to your course on television, on radio, in newspapers and in podcasts.

2 Make sure you know how to cope if you have a serious problem.
  a) Check your centre's procedures so you know who to talk to in a crisis, and who to contact if that person is absent.

  b) Find out where you can get hold of a copy of the main procedures in your centre that might affect you if you have a serious problem. Then read them.

Activity: Coping with problems

Another night, another argument – Tracey's parents are at it again. Last night, it was her mum shouting at her dad for being out late; tonight it's an argument over the washing-up. Tracey's mum has had enough and has threatened to leave her dad. The way things are going, Tracey is worried that her mum will actually leave.

When Tracey started her BTEC Level 3 National in Floristry, her parents were overjoyed. They could see that she had found something that was really interesting and with great job prospects, including her ultimate dream of running her own business.

Now Tracey is in her second year of the course and is really struggling. She still likes the course, but she finds it so hard to focus, and her work is starting to suffer. Can you suggest four things that Tracey can do to help her through the situation and allow her to do well on her course?

1.	
2.	
3.	
4.	

AND FINALLY ...

Refer to this Study Skills Guide whenever you need to remind yourself about something related to your course. Keep it in a safe place so that you can use it whenever you need to refresh your memory. That way, you'll get the very best out of your course – and yourself!

TOP TIP

The time and effort you will be putting into this course deserves to be rewarded. Make sure you know how to confront and successfully overcome problems.

Skills building

This section has been written to help you improve the skills needed to do your best in your assignments. You may be excellent at some skills already, others may need further work. The skills you can expect to demonstrate on your course include:

- your personal, learning and thinking skills (**PLTS**)
- your **functional skills** of ICT, maths/numeracy and English
- your proofreading and document production skills.

Personal, learning and thinking skills (PLTS)

These are the skills, personal qualities and behaviour that enable you to operate more independently, work more confidently with other people and be more effective at work. You'll develop these on your BTEC Level 3 National course through a variety of experiences and as you take on different roles and responsibilities.

> The skills are divided into six groups.
>
> 1 **Independent enquirers** can process and evaluate information they investigate from different perspectives. They can plan what to do and how to do it, and take into account the consequences of making different decisions.
>
> 2 **Creative thinkers** generate and explore different ideas. They make connections between ideas, events and experiences that enable them to be inventive and imaginative.
>
> 3 **Reflective learners** can assess themselves and other people. They can evaluate their own strengths and limitations. They set themselves realistic goals, monitor their own performance and welcome feedback.
>
> 4 **Team workers** collaborate with other people to achieve common goals. They are fair and considerate to others, whether as a team leader or team member, and take account of different opinions.
>
> 5 **Self-managers** are well-organised and show personal responsibility, initiative, creativity and enterprise. They look for new challenges and responsibilities and are flexible when priorities change.
>
> 6 **Effective participators** play a full part in the life of their school, college, workplace or wider community by taking responsible action to bring improvements for others as well as themselves.

Action points

1 Many parts of this Study Skills Guide relate to the development of your own personal, learning and thinking skills. For each of the following, suggest the main skill groups to which the chapter relates. Refer to the box above and write a number next to each chapter title below.

a) Use your time wisely. _____

b) Understand how to research and analyse information. _____

c) Work productively as a member of a group. _____

d) Understand yourself. _____

e) Utilise all your resources. _____

f) Maximise your opportunities and manage your problems. _____

2 You have been on your BTEC National course for a few months now and, although everyone is enjoying the work, you realise that some of the learners have complaints.

First, several learners object to an increase in the price of printouts and photocopying, on the basis that they can't do good work for their assignments if this is too expensive. You disagree and think that the prices are reasonable, given the cost of paper.

Second, a timetable change means your 2 pm – 4 pm Friday afternoon class has been moved to 9 am – 11 am. Some learners are annoyed and want it changed back, while others are delighted.

a) For the first problem, identify four factors which could indicate that those complaining about the price rise might be justified.

1

2

3

4

b) Now consider the second problem.

   i) Think about which learners in your group would be most affected by the timetable change. Who might be most disturbed? Who might benefit from the earlier start?

   ii) Try to think of a creative solution, or compromise, that would please both groups.

c) During the discussions about these issues, some quieter members of the class are often shouted down by the more excitable members. Suggest a strategy for dealing with this, which everyone is likely to accept.

You can also check your ideas with the suggestions given on page 95.

3 a) Complete the chart opposite, identifying occasions when you may need to demonstrate personal, learning and thinking skills in your future career. Alternatively, apply each area to a part-time job you are currently doing.

b) Identify areas where you think you are quite strong and put a tick in the 'S' column. Check that you could provide evidence to support this judgement, such as a time when you have demonstrated this skill.

c) Now consider areas where you are not so good and put a cross in the 'W' column.

d) Then practise self-management by identifying two appropriate goals to achieve over the next month and make a note of them in the space provided. If possible, talk through your ideas at your next individual tutorial.

Personal, learning and thinking skills for future career/current part-time job				
Skill group	**Example skills**	**Occasions when you use/ will use skill**	**S**	**W**
Independent enquirers	Finding information Solving problems Making decisions Reconciling conflicting information or views Justifying decisions			
Creative thinkers	Finding imaginative solutions Making original connections Finding new ways to do something Opportunities for being innovative and inventive			
Reflective learners	Goals you may set yourself Reviewing your own progress Encouraging feedback Dealing with setbacks or criticism			
Team workers	Working with others Coping with different views to your own Adapting your behaviour Being fair and considerate			
Self-managers	Being self-starting and showing initiative Dealing positively with changing priorities Organising your own time and resources Dealing with pressure Managing your emotions			
Effective participators	Identifying issues of concern to others Proposing ways forward Identifying improvements for others Influencing other people Putting forward a persuasive argument			
Goals	1			
	2			

Functional skills

Functional skills are practical skills that everyone needs to have in order to study and work effectively. They involve using and applying English, maths and ICT.

Improving your literacy skills

Your written English communication skills

A good vocabulary increases your ability to explain yourself clearly. Work that is presented without spelling and punctuation errors looks professional, and increases the likelihood of someone understanding your intended meaning. Your written communication skills will be tested in many assignments. You should work at improving areas of weakness, such as spelling, punctuation or vocabulary.

Try the following ideas to help you improve your written communication skills.

- Read more as this introduces you to new words, and it will help your spelling.
- Look up new words in a dictionary and try to use them in conversation.
- Use a Thesaurus (you can access one electronically in Word) to find alternatives to words you use a lot, this adds variety to your work.
- Never use words you don't understand in the hope that they sound impressive.
- Write neatly, so people can read what you've written.
- Do crosswords to improve your word power and spelling.
- Improve your punctuation – especially the use of apostrophes – either by using an online programme or by using a communication textbook.
- Go to page 96 to find out how to gain access to some helpful websites for this page.

Verbal and non-verbal communication (NVC) skills

Talking appropriately means using the right words and 'tone'; using the right body language means sending positive signals to reinforce this message – such as smiling at someone when you say 'Hello'. Both verbal and non-verbal communication skills are essential when dealing with people at work.

The following ideas are some hints for successful communication.

- Be polite, tactful and sensitive to other people's feelings.
- Think about the words and phrases that you like to hear, and use them when communicating with other people.
- Use simple language so that people can understand you easily. Explain what you mean, when necessary.
- Speak at the right pace. Don't speak so slowly that everyone loses interest, or so fast that no-one can understand you.
- Speak loudly enough for people to hear you clearly – but don't shout!
- Think about the specific needs of different people – whether you are talking to a senior manager, an important client, a shy colleague or an angry customer.
- Recognise the importance of non-verbal communication (NVC) so that you send positive signals by smiling, making eye contact, giving an encouraging nod or leaning forwards to show interest.
- Read other people's body language to spot if they are anxious or impatient so that you can react appropriately.

TOP TIP

Make sure you use the right tone for the person you're talking to. Would you talk to an adult in the same way you'd talk to a very young child?

Action points

1 TGo to page 94 to find out how to gain access to websites which can help you to improve your literacy skills.

2 A battery made in China contained the following information.

> **DO NOT CONNECT IMPROPERLY**
>
> **CHARGE OR DISPOSE OF IN FIRE**

a) Can you see any problems with this? Give a reason for your answer.

b) Reword the information so that it is unambiguous.

3 If you ever thought you could completely trust the spellchecker on your computer, type the text given in box A on the next page into your computer. Your spellchecker will not highlight a single error; yet even at a glance you should be able to spot dozens of errors!

Read the passage in box A and try to understand it. Then rewrite it in box B on the next page without spelling, grammatical or punctuation errors. Compare your finished work with the suggested version on page 95.

Box A

Anyone desirable to write books or reports, be they short or long, should strive too maximise they're optimal use of one's English grammar and obliviously there is an need for correct spelling two one should not neglect punctuation neither.

Frequent lea, many people and individuals become confusing or just do not no it, when righting, when words that mean different, when sounding identically, or when pronounced very similar, are knot too bee spelled inn the same whey. The quay two suck seeding is dew care, a lack off witch Leeds too Miss Spellings that mite otherwise of bean a voided. Spell chequers donut find awl missed takes.

Despite all the pitfalls how ever, with practise, patients and the right altitude, any one can soon become a grate writer and speaker, as what I did.

Box B Now rewrite the passage in the space below without errors.

4 In each of the statements listed in the table below suggest what the body language described might mean.

Statement	What might this body language mean?
a) You are talking to your manager when he steps away from you and crosses his arms over his chest.	
b) You are talking to your friend about what she did at the weekend but she's avoiding making eye contact with you.	
c) During a tutorial session, your tutor is constantly tapping his fingers on the arm of his chair.	
d) Whenever you talk to your friend about your next assignment, she bites her lower lip.	

Improving your maths or numeracy skills

If you think numeracy isn't relevant to you, then think again! Numeracy is an essential life skill. If you can't carry out basic calculations accurately then you will have problems, perhaps when you least expect them. You'll often encounter numbers in various contexts – sometimes they will be correctly given, sometimes not. Unless you have a basic understanding about numeracy, you won't be able to tell the difference.

Good numeracy skills will improve your ability to express yourself, especially in assignments and at work. If you have problems, there are strategies that you can practise to help:

- Try to do basic calculations in your head, then check them on a calculator.
- Ask your tutor for help if important calculations give you problems.
- When you are using your computer, use the onscreen calculator (or a spreadsheet package) to do calculations.
- Investigate puzzle sites and brain training software, such as Dr Kageyama's Maths Training by Nintendo.

Action points

1 Go to page 94 to find out how to gain access to websites which can help you to improve your numeracy skills.

2 Try the following task with a friend or family member.

Each of you should write down 36 simple calculations in a list, eg

8 × 6, 19 − 8, 14 + 6.

Exchange lists. See who can answer the most calculations correctly in the shortest time.

3 Figures aren't always what they appear to be. For example, Sophie watches *Who Wants To Be a Millionaire?* She hears Chris Tarrant say

that there have been over 500 shows, with 1200 contestants who have each won over £50,000 on average. Five people have won £1 million.

Sophie says she is going to enter because she is almost certain to win more than £50,000 and could even win a million pounds.

a) On the figures given, what is the approximate total of money won over 500 shows (to the nearest £ million)?

b) Assuming that Sophie is chosen to appear on the show, and makes it on air as a contestant, do you think Sophie's argument that she will 'almost certainly' win more than £50,000 is correct? Give a reason for your answer.

(The correct answer is on page 96.)

4 You have a part-time job and have been asked to carry out a survey on the usage of the drinks vending machine. You decide to survey 500 people, and find that:

- 225 use the machine to buy one cup of coffee per day only
- 100 use the machine to buy one cup of tea per day only
- 75 use the machine to buy one cup of cold drink per day only
- 50 use the machine to buy one cup of hot chocolate per day only
- the rest are non-users
- the ratio of male to female users is 2:1.

a) How many men in your survey use the machine?

b) How many women in your survey use the machine?

c) Calculate the proportion of the people in your survey that use the machine.

Express this as a fraction and as a percentage.

d) What is the ratio of coffee drinkers to tea drinkers in your survey?

e) What is the ratio of coffee drinkers to hot chocolate drinkers in your survey?

f) If people continue to purchase from the machine in the same ratio found in your survey, and last month 1800 cups of coffee were sold, what would you expect the sales of the cold drinks to be?

g) Using the answer to f), if coffee costs 65p and all cold drinks cost 60p, how much would have been spent in total last month on these two items?

Improving your ICT skills

Good ICT skills are an asset in many aspects of your daily life and not just for those studying to be IT practitioners.

These are ways in which you can improve your ICT skills.

- Check that you can use the main features of the software packages you need to produce your assignments, eg Word, Excel and PowerPoint.

- Choose a good search engine and learn to use it properly. For more information, go to page 96 to find out how to access a useful website.

- Developing and using your IT skills enables you to enhance your assignments. This may include learning how to import and export text and artwork from one package to another; taking digital photographs and inserting them into your work and/or creating drawings or diagrams by using appropriate software.

Action points

1 Check your basic knowledge of IT terminology by identifying each of these items on your computer screen:

a) taskbar

b) toolbar

c) title bar

d) menu bar

e) mouse pointer

f) scroll bars

g) status bar

h) insertion point

i) maximise/ minimise button.

2 Assess your IT skills by identifying the packages and operations you find easy to use and those that you find more difficult. If you use Microsoft Office products (Word, PowerPoint, Access or Excel) you can find out more about improving your skills online. Go to page 96 to find out how to access a useful website for this action points section.

3 Search the internet to find a useful dictionary of IT terms. Bookmark it for future use. Find out the meaning of any of the following terms that you don't know already:

a) portal

b) cached link

c) home page

d) browser

e) firewall

f) HTML

g) URL

h) cookie

i) hyperlink

j) freeware.

Proofreading and document preparation skills

Improving your keyboard, document production and general IT skills can save you hours of time. When you have good skills, the work you produce will be of a far more professional standard.

- Think about learning to touch-type. Your centre may have a workshop you can join, or you can use an online program – go to page 94 to find out how to access a web link for this section. From here you can access websites that will allow you to test and work on improving your typing skills.

- Obtain correct examples of any document formats you will have to use, such as a report or summary, either from your tutor, the internet or from a textbook.

- Proofread all your work carefully. A spellchecker won't find all your mistakes, so you must read through it yourself as well.

- Make sure your work looks professional by using a suitable typeface and font size, as well as reasonable margins.

- Print your work and store the printouts neatly, so that it stays in perfect condition for when you hand it in.

Action points

1 You can check and improve your typing skills using online typing sites – see link in previous section.

2 Check your ability to create documents by scoring yourself out of 5 for each of the following questions, where 5 is something you can do easily and 0 is something you can't do at all. Then focus on improving every score where you rated yourself 3 or less.

I know how to:

a) create a new document and open a saved document _____

b) use the mouse to click, double-click and drag objects _____

c) use drop-down menus _____

d) customise my toolbars by adding or deleting options _____

e) save and/or print a document _____

f) create folders and sub-folders to organise my work _____

g) move a folder I use regularly to My Places _____

h) amend text in a document _____

i) select, copy, paste and delete information in a document _____

j) quickly find and replace text in a document _____

k) insert special characters _____

l) create a table or insert a diagram in a document _____

m) change the text size, font and colour _____

n) add bold, italics or underscore _____

o) create a bullet or numbered list _____

p) align text left, right or centred _____

q) format pages before they are printed _____

r) proofread a document so that there are no mistakes _____.

Answers

Activity: Let's give you a tip... (page 72)

a) i) Fact

ii) Opinion – the number cannot be validated

iii) Fact

iv) Opinion

v) Opinion

vi) Opinion – again the number is estimated

Skills building answers

PLTS action points (page 85)

1 a) Use your time wisely = **5** Self-managers

b) Understand how to research and analyse information = **1** Independent enquirers, **5** Self-managers

c) Work productively as a member of a group = **4** Team workers, **6** Effective participators

d) Understand yourself = **3** Reflective learners

e) Utilise all your resources = **5** Self-managers

f) Maximise your opportunities and manage your problems = **1** Independent enquirers, **2** Creative thinkers, **3** Reflective learners, **5** Self-managers

2 a) Factors to consider in relation to the increased photocopying/printing charges include: the comparative prices charged by other schools/colleges, how often there is a price rise, whether any printing or photocopying at all can be done without charge, whether there are any concessions for special tasks or assignments, the availability of class sets of books/popular library books for loan (which reduces the need for photocopying).

b) i) An earlier start will be more likely to negatively affect those who live further away and who are reliant on public transport, particularly in rural areas. The earlier finish will benefit anyone who has a part-time job that starts on a Friday afternoon or who has after college commitments, such as looking after younger sisters or brothers.

ii) The scope for compromise would depend on whether there are any classes between 11 am and 2 pm on a Friday, whether tutors had any flexibility and whether the new 9 am – 11 am class could be moved to another time or day.

c) One strategy would be to allow discussion for a set time, ensure everyone had spoken, then put the issue to a vote. The leader should prompt suggestions from quieter members by asking people individually what they think.

Literacy skills action points (page 89)

2 a) The statement reads as if it is acceptable to either charge it or dispose of it in fire.

b) Do not connect this battery improperly. Do not recharge it and do not dispose of it in fire.

3 Anyone who wishes to write books or reports, whether short or long, should try to use English grammatically. Obviously there is a need for correct spelling, too. Punctuation should also not be neglected.

Frequently, people confuse words with different meanings when they are writing, especially when these sound identical or very similar, even when they must not be spelled in the same way. The key to succeeding is due care, a lack of which leads to misspellings that might otherwise have been avoided. Spellcheckers do not find all mistakes.

Despite all the pitfalls, however, with practice, patience and the right attitude, anyone can soon become a great writer and speaker, like me.

4 Possible answers.

a) Stepping backwards and crossing arms across the chest might indicate that you manager is creating a barrier between you and himself. This may be because he is angry with you.

b) Your friend may be feeling guilty about what she did at the weekend, or not confident that you will approve of what she tells you.

c) Your tutor might be frustrated as he has many things to do and so wants the tutorial to finish quickly.

d) Your friend might be anxious about the next assignment or about the time she has to complete it.

Numeracy action points (page 92)

3 a) £60 million

b) Sophie's argument is incorrect as £50, 000 is an average, i.e. some contestants will win more, but many will win much less. The distribution of prize money is greater at lower amounts because more people win small amounts of money than large amounts – and only five contestants have won the top prize of £1 million.

4 a) 300

b) 150

c) 9/10ths, 90%

d) 225:100 (= 45:20) = 9:4

e) 225:50 = 9:2

f) 600

g) £1530

Accessing website links

Links to various websites are referred to throughout this BTEC Level 3 National Study Skills Guide. To ensure that these links are up-to-date, that they work and that the sites aren't inadvertently linked to any material that could be considered offensive, we have made the links available on our website: www.pearsonhotlinks.co.uk. When you visit the site, search for this title BTEC Level 3 National Study Skills Guide in Land and Environment or ISBN 9781846909276. From here you can gain access to the website links and information on how they can be used to help you with your studies.

Useful terms

Accreditation of Prior Learning (APL)
Some of your previous achievements and experiences may be able to be used to count towards your qualification.

Apprenticeships
Schemes that enable you to work and earn money at the same time as you gain further qualifications (an NVQ award and a technical certificate) and improve your functional skills. Apprentices learn work-based skills relevant to their job role and their chosen industry. See page 96 for how you can access a website to find out more.

Assessment methods
Techniques used to check that your work demonstrates the learning and understanding required for your qualification, such as assignments, case studies and practical tasks.

Assessor
An assessor is the tutor who marks or assesses your work.

Assignment
A complex task or mini-project set to meet specific grading criteria and learning outcomes.

Awarding body
An organisation responsible for devising, assessing and issuing qualifications. The awarding body for all BTEC qualifications is Edexcel.

Credit value
The number of credits attached to your BTEC course. The credit value increases in relation to the length of time you need to complete the course, from 30 credits for a BTEC Level 3 Certificate, 60 credits for a Subsidiary Diploma, 120 credits for a Diploma, up to 180 credits for an Extended Diploma.

Degrees
Higher education qualifications offered by universities and colleges. Foundation degrees take two years to complete; honours degrees may take three years or longer.

Department for Business Innovation and Skills (BIS)
BIS is responsible for further and higher education and skills training, as well as functions related to trade and industry. See page 96 for how you can access a website to find out more.

Department for Education
The Department for Education is responsible for schools and education, as well as children's services. See page 96 for how you can access a website to find out more.

Distance learning
When you learn and/or study for a qualification at home or at work. You communicate with your tutor and/or the centre that organises the course by post, by telephone or electronically.

Educational Maintenance Award (EMA)
An EMA is a means-tested award that provides eligible learners under 19 who are studying a full-time course at school or college with a cash sum of money every week. See page 96 for how you can access a website to find out more.

External verification
Formal checking of the programme by an Edexcel representative that focuses on sampling various assignments to check content, accurate assessment and grading.

Forbidden combinations
There are some qualifications that cannot be taken simultaneously because their content is too similar.

Functional skills
Practical skills in English, maths and ICT that enable people to work confidently, effectively and independently. Level 2 Functional Skills are mapped to the units of BTEC Level 3 National qualifications. They aren't compulsory to achieve on the course, but are of great use.

Grade boundaries
Pre-set points that determine whether you will achieve a pass, merit or distinction as the overall final grade(s) for your qualification.

Grading criteria

The specific evidence you have to demonstrate to obtain a particular grade in the unit.

Grading domains

The main areas of learning that support the learning outcomes. On a BTEC Level 3 National course these are: application of knowledge and understanding; development of practical and technical skills; personal development for occupational roles; application of PLTS and functional skills.

Grading grid

The table in each unit of your qualification specification that sets out what you have to show you can do.

Higher education (HE)

Post-secondary and post-further education, usually provided by universities and colleges.

Higher-level skills

These are skills such as evaluating or critically assessing information. They are more difficult than lower-level skills such as writing a description or making a list. You must be able to demonstrate higher-level skills to achieve a distinction.

Indicative reading

Recommended books and journals whose content is both suitable and relevant for the BTEC unit studied.

Induction

A short programme of events at the start of a course designed to give you essential information and introduce you to your fellow learners and tutors, so that you can settle down as quickly and easily as possible.

Internal verification

The quality checks carried out by nominated tutors at your school or college to ensure that all assignments are at the right level and cover appropriate learning outcomes and grading criteria, and that all assessors are marking work consistently and to the same standard.

Investors in People (IiP)

A national quality standard that sets a level of good practice for training and developing of people within a business. Participating organisations must demonstrate commitment to achieving the standard.

Learning outcomes

The knowledge and skills you must demonstrate to show that you have effectively learned a unit.

Learning support

Additional help that is available to all learners in a school or college who have learning difficulties or other special needs.

Levels of study

The depth, breadth and complexity of knowledge, understanding and skills required to achieve a qualification, which also determine its level. Level 2 equates to GCSE level and Level 3 equates to A-level. As you successfully achieve one level, you can then progress to the next. BTEC qualifications are offered at Entry Level, then Levels 1, 2, 3, 4 and 5.

Local Education Authority (LEA)

The local government body responsible for providing education for all learners of compulsory school age. The LEA is also responsible for managing the education budget for 16–19-year-old learners in its area.

Mandatory units

These are units that all learners must complete to gain a qualification, in this case a BTEC Level 3 National. Some BTEC qualifications have an over-arching title, eg Construction, but within Construction you can choose different pathways. Your chosen pathway may have additional mandatory units specific to that pathway.

Mentor

A more experienced person who will guide you and counsel you if you have a problem or difficulty.

Mode of delivery

The way in which a qualification is offered to learners, for example part-time, full-time, as a short course or by distance learning.

National Occupational Standard (NOS)

Statements of the skills, knowledge and understanding you need to develop in order to be competent at a particular job.

National Vocational Qualification (NVQ)

Qualifications that concentrate on the practical skills and knowledge required to do a job competently. They are usually assessed in the workplace and range from Level 1 (the lowest) to Level 5 (the highest).

Nested qualifications

Qualifications that have 'common' units, so that learners can easily progress from one to another by adding on more units

Ofqual

The public body responsible for regulating qualifications, exams and tests in England.

Optional units

Units on your course from which you may be able to make a choice. They help you specialise your skills, knowledge and understanding, and may help progression into work or further education.

Pathway

All BTEC Level 3 National qualifications comprise a small number of mandatory units and a larger number of optional units. These units are grouped into different combinations to provide alternative pathways to achieving the qualification. These pathways are usually linked to different career preferences.

Peer review

This involves feedback on your performance by your peers (members of your team or class group.) You will also be given an opportunity to review their performance.

Plagiarism

The practice of copying someone else's work or work from any other sources (eg the internet), and passing it off as your own. This practice is strictly forbidden on all courses.

Personal, learning and thinking skills (PLTS)

The skills, personal qualities and behaviour that improve your ability to work independently. Developing these skills makes you more effective and confident at work. Opportunities for developing these skills are a feature of all BTEC Level 3 National courses. These skills aren't compulsory to achieve on the course, but are of great use to you.

Portfolio

A collection of work compiled by a learner, usually as evidence of learning, to present to an assessor.

Procrastinator

Someone who is forever putting off or delaying work, either because they are lazy or because they have poor organisational skills.

Professional body

An organisation that exists to promote or support a particular profession, for example the Royal Institute of British Architects (RIBA).

Professional development and training

This involves undertaking activities relevant to your job to increase and/or update your knowledge and skills.

Project

A project is a comprehensive piece of work, which normally involves original research and investigation by an individual or by a team. The findings and results may be presented in writing and summarised as a presentation.

Qualifications and Credit Framework (QCF)

The QCF is a framework for recognising skills and qualifications. It does this by awarding credit for qualifications and units so that they are easier to measure and compare. All BTEC Level 3 National qualifications are part of the QCF.

Qualifications and Curriculum Development Agency (QCDA)

The QCDA is responsible for maintaining and developing the national curriculum, delivering assessments, tests and examinations, and reforming qualifications.

Quality assurance

In education, this is the process of continually checking that a course of study is meeting the specific requirements set down by the awarding body.

Sector Skills Councils (SSCs)

The 25 employer-led, independent organisations responsible for improving workforce skills in the UK by identifying skill gaps and improving learning in the workplace. Each council covers a different type of industry.

Semester

Many universities and colleges divide their academic year into two halves or semesters, one from September to January and one from February to July.

Seminar

A learning event involving a group of learners and a tutor, which may be learner-led, and may follow research into a topic that has been introduced at an earlier stage.

Study buddy

A person in your group or class who takes notes for you and keeps you informed of important developments if you are absent. You do the same for them in return.

Time-constrained assignment

An assessment you must complete within a fixed time limit.

Tutorial

An individual or small group meeting with your tutor at which you can discuss your current work and other more general course issues. At an individual tutorial, your progress on the course will be discussed and you can raise any concerns or personal worries you may have.

The University and Colleges Admissions Service (UCAS)

UCAS (pronounced 'you-cass') is the central organisation that processes all applications for higher education (HE) courses.

UCAS points

The number of points allocated by UCAS for the qualifications you have obtained. Higher education institutions specify how many points you need to be accepted on the courses they offer. See page 96 for how you can access a website to find out more.

Unit abstract

The summary at the start of each BTEC unit that tells you what the unit is about.

Unit content

Details about the topics covered by the unit and the knowledge and skills you need to complete it.

Unit points

The number of points you gain when you complete a unit. These will depend on the grade you achieve (pass, merit or distinction).

Vocational qualification

Designed to develop knowledge and understanding relevant to a chosen area of work.

Work experience

Time you spend on an employer's premises when you learn about the enterprise, carry out work-based tasks, and develop skills and knowledge.

Please note that all information given within these useful terms was correct at the time of going to print.